James E. Thorold Rogers

Historical Gleanings

A series of sketches: Wiklif, Laud, Wilkes, Horne, Tooke. Second series

James E. Thorold Rogers

Historical Gleanings

A series of sketches: Wiklif, Laud, Wilkes, Horne, Tooke. Second series

ISBN/EAN: 9783337012465

Printed in Europe, USA, Canada, Australia, Japan

Cover: Foto ©ninafisch / pixelio.de

More available books at **www.hansebooks.com**

HISTORICAL GLEANINGS

SECOND SERIES

HISTORICAL GLEANINGS

A SERIES OF SKETCHES

WIKLIF. LAUD. WILKES.
HORNE TOOKE.

BY

JAMES E. THOROLD ROGERS

Second Series

Cœnæ fercula nostræ
Mallem convivis quam placuisse coquis.

London
MACMILLAN AND CO.
1870

[*All rights reserved*]

PREFACE.

The Essays contained in this Second Series were written with the same purpose as those which have been already published, and on the same plan. They are lectures, in which it has been my object to state the social facts of the time in which the individual, whose history is handled, took part in public business. Hence, as before, each person is introduced to my reader with a prefatory account of certain circumstances which influenced society at the time.

Three of the men whose place in history I have attempted to expound were ecclesiastics. But I have not referred, except in so far as it was necessary for me to do so, to the theological tenets which they entertained. Two of these ecclesiastics were notably political clergymen; by which I mean, that they used the authority of their function in order to disseminate or enforce their political theories. The third was only historically a clergyman, for the greater part of his public life was justified on the protest which he energetically and perpetually made —that his clerical antecedents did not extinguish his civil rights. His protest was disregarded and rebutted, and, in my opinion, with the most important and decisive consequences. The career of Wilkes is closely connected with that of Horne Tooke, and, in many particulars, is in marked contrast to it.

My reader will find that I have consulted the common sources of information for the history of three among the subjects comprised in this series. But I may perhaps say, that though I have used the Chronicles, and such comments on the works and life of Wiklif as have been published, my researches into the social life of Englishmen during the fourteenth century have supplied me with some advantages for dealing with the times of the great English Reformer.

JAMES E. THOROLD ROGERS.

OXFORD, *December* 22, 1869.

CONTENTS.

	PAGE
JOHN WIKLIF	1
WILLIAM LAUD	65
JOHN WILKES	129
JOHN HORNE TOOKE	187

JOHN WIKLIF.

B

JOHN WIKLIF.

AT no time perhaps in the history of the world has personal influence, as contrasted with official authority, availed so much as through the course of the thirteenth and fourteenth centuries. There is a short period during the later years of the Roman republic in which a somewhat similar phenomenon was witnessed. But the resemblance is merely external. The machinery of civil government had broken down in Rome. Its military system was in full vigour, and remained vigorous for two centuries after the Roman people had become a greedy and disorganised rabble, the prey of the most daring and sagacious adventurer. But the social system of Europe was in course of construction during the period to which I refer. Side by side of and ultimately in substitution for that narrow theory of military reciprocity which we know as the feudal rule, grew a host of independent institutions, sometimes in sharp conflict, sometimes in harmony. But the alternate vigour or decline of these institutions depended constantly on the capacity or incapacity of those who represented or sustained them. Men had not yet learned to recognise the office and to excuse or condone the incapacity of the official. When the king was weak, the royal power waned; but, on the other hand, a vigorous monarch might make himself well nigh absolute. So a university rose and fell with the reputation of its teachers. Even the higher courts of law, in the midst of a system under which nearly all justice was administered in nearly every village, were resorted to at discretion, for the vindication of private rights, as the judge was thought competent. The influence of the national clergy, secular or regular, (as the minister of religion was called, according as he entered on parochial duty, or enrolled himself under some monastic rule,) depended greatly on the personal reputation of the individual or the order. It is an observation of Machiavelli, that the influence of the preaching of SS. Dominic and Francis, the founders of the Dominican and Franciscan rule respectively, brought about a great reformation, and notably enhanced the authority of the clergy. It was principally through the Church, too, that poor men often rose to eminent place, and founded a family in the person of some collateral kinsman. In time of war, a military career was also open to the diligent and adventurous. Some at least of Edward the Third's captains were men of ignoble origin.

In point of fact, medieval Europe possessed nothing, in the municipal government of the several monarchies which composed it, of what we call centralisation. The towns gained charters of self-government. The court of every manor exercised a vigorous jurisdiction over those who were in feudal subordination to the lord. The abbeys obtained exemption from the visitation and discipline of the bishops. The universities, which had been founded chiefly by and almost exclusively for churchmen, looked upon any interference whatever, on the part of the hierarchy, with jealousy, and resisted all extraneous jurisdiction with determination. Their numerous students (for they formed the public schools of the Middle Ages) cared little for legate or bishop, but petitioned and procured abundant charters and franchises from the highest secular authorities. In England especially, this system of local self-government had full play. As might be expected from such a tone of public feeling, the police of each local jurisdiction was vigilant and active. Nor was this spirit of peculiar independence mere anarchy or disorganisation. It was a process out of which, by the conflict of social and political forces, a system of public law and administrative government was gradually developed, in which as much as possible of self-government was preserved; of which more would have been preserved, had it not been for the rise of monarchical power at the conclusion of the fifteenth century. This power suspended in some countries and annihilated in others the earlier distribution of political power, of peculiar jurisdiction.

To this requirement, that political and social influence should depend on personal and individual character, there was at that time one memorable and eminent exception. The papacy was a real and a prodigious force, exercised independently of the character or capacity of the individual who occupied the papal chair. Its empire was unchallenged. It had been a living, a vigorous, an acknowledged authority before any royal house in Europe had been founded. Christianity had overthrown Paganism. It had absorbed the traditions of the Roman empire. It had composed and practised an elaborate code of law, how or with what motive constructed we need not inquire, at a time when every European nation was not only without a written law, but regulated its domestic affairs by barbarous rules and customs. Popes might be imprisoned, dethroned, poisoned; might be weak, profligate, rapacious; but the administrative powers of the Court of Rome secured it the obedience of its spiritual subjects, and accumulated its influence in the Western world. Real loyalty was entertained towards the papacy, though varying in its degree, for it was more fervid as Rome was more remote from her spiritual dependencies.

It is the custom with many persons who have commented on the singular relation in which an Italian prelate, elected by the ecclesiastical life-peers of a small state in Central Italy, stood to the monarchs, the nobles, and the peoples of Western Europe, to assign the great influence of the papacy to the effect of audacity on the one hand, and superstition on the other. I am convinced that this explanation is superficial and unreal. I hope I may not be misunderstood when I say that there must always be some audacity in the maintenance of any ecclesiastical authority or influence whatsoever, and that what those who dissent from such authority or influence call arrogance, can always be charged, rightly or wrongly, against all spiritual rulers, and even all religious reformers. But unless religious impulses are degraded to the terrors which savages feel at magic or witchcraft, and an artful priesthood plays on these terrors, the reasonable adherence to any system of religion, however erroneous it may seem to us, is always based on a persuasion that its offices are generally, and profess to be universally, beneficent. It was when the policy of the papacy was believed to be sordid, and dictated by plans of petty aggrandisement, that its influence declined.

I make no doubt that some part of its authority was due to its prestige. For example, the papacy had rooted out the race of the most powerful and able prince that Europe had seen since the days of Charles the Great. Identifying itself with the cause of Italian liberty, it had crushed the house of Suabia. Again, the most fertile and prosperous province of what is now called France, had revolted from its spiritual allegiance to the faith of Rome, and the kingdom of Toulouse had been wasted by Montfort, at the bidding of the pope. It should be remembered that in the period to which I refer, the papacy, among other expedients for maintaining its authority, had adopted the policy and employed the agencies of the Mohammedan conquerors of the East; and we need not be told, that religious fanaticism, honestly embraced or entertained, makes armies invincible. Nor do I forget that when there is no nationality, and therefore nothing of what is called patriotism, the craving of men after a system of social union disposes them to look outside the mere state in which they live.

In our own time, as the governments of Europe have become more just and more liberal, and therefore as their authority becomes less palpable, the sense of nationality, of local patriotism, has again been weakened, and the various nations of Europe are beginning to discuss the question as to whether their interests are really furthered by the prodigious armies which governments maintain, apparently in order to preserve intact certain arbitrary boundaries. Hence, partly as a reaction against the existing system, partly because all people yearn after a political unity, the question whether Europe may not hereafter become a federation of autonomous states is growing in importance, and may soon arrive at an affirmative solution.

But in the thirteenth and fourteenth centuries Europe had no nationalities. A monarchy was a precarious and shifting suzerainty over provinces bound together by no closer tie than the monarch's inheritance. In the latter half of the twelfth century, Henry the Second of England, apart from such real or presumed authority as he exercised or claimed over these islands, held the uncontested inheritance of the whole seaboard of France. But such a monarchy was a mere geographical quantity. Its political cohesion was that of a rope of sand. It was held loosely together by Richard. It was lost by John. It was regained in part by Edward the First. Its fairest regions were recovered, and confirmed by treaty to Edward the Third, to be lost finally by the same monarch at the close of his reign. The House of Lancaster claimed by descent or conquest France and Castile, but, after a transient success, was constrained to be contented with a barren title. In fact, a medieval kingdom had no history, it had no inveterate traditions, by which, more than anything else, nations form political unities. Had it not been for the independence of those societies to which I have already referred, it would have had no more solidity than an Eastern monarchy has. And here I may perhaps remind my hearers that, notwithstanding the barbarous code of law, the coarse despotism, the indolence, sensuality, and violence which are the characteristics of the several Mohammedan governments of the world, they gain no little cohesion and vitality by their recognition of a central unity in the chief of Islam. In the absence of a real nationality, then, the peoples of medieval Europe found a centre of union in the spiritual empire of the pope, who, after the humiliation of the German empire, appeared to be the most majestic potentate of Western Europe.

Now it was this spectacle of authority which riveted the imagination and challenged the admiration of Europe five centuries ago. Here was an institution, believed to be divine, and vindicating in the minds of men no small part of such a reverence, because its scope lay far above the petty dynastic squabbles in which European monarchs were generally engaged. It is hard for us, in the midst of our modern associations, to realise the intensity with which medieval Europe adhered to what it conceived to be the pillar of Christianity, the barrier against oppression or slavery. But, I repeat, the energy with which men cling to the representative of social unity is always most keen when municipal unity or nationality is weak or undeveloped. We may guess at its vigour by seeing how men shunned the imputation of disloyalty to such a received institution. In the Middle Ages, the charge of heresy was far more dangerous, far more deeply dreaded, than that of treason. Men whom we call weak, because in the face of their convictions they recanted opinions which they had honestly expressed, were far more affected by the dread of excommunication than they were by the penalties of local justice. Something of this feeling was, perhaps still is, felt in Spain, where, owing to historical causes on which I need not dwell, men who abandon every other obligation, are restrained by the dread of being accounted wanting in orthodoxy. In these days, we should call these fears superstitious. But let no one imagine, that if he had lived in the times I speak of, he could have easily escaped their contagion, or could have boldly defied a power whose authority seemed so vast, and whose prestige was so majestic.

Nor was this allegiance based on causes which are wholly unintelligible to modern habits of thought. Rome was undoubtedly for many a year the real barrier against oppression. She took part, in the better days of her political ascendancy, with the general interests of humanity. She did her best to discourage slavery. She constantly interposed to check the violence of feudal quarrels. She exercised an international influence in preserving a balance of power, in proclaiming the Truce of God, in enforcing a cessation from dynastic wars. She did something towards developing a public conscience in the affairs of nations. Her administration of justice was slow but pure; else her courts would never have been frequented. It was, among other and minor reasons, to make these courts more accessible to her clients, that she took a fatal step in the beginning of the fourteenth century.

The popes were rapacious, and levied heavy taxes on the European nations who acknowledged them. They appointed their dependants to benefices in

England and elsewhere, and dispensed with all duties, even that of residence—a dispensation often convenient to the reputation of the Church. They claimed an absolute right of appeal in all ecclesiastical cases, and it was not difficult to turn this right of appeal into a right of patronage. Complaints, indeed, against this perpetual interference are also perpetual. But the complaint was against the pope, not against the papacy. The abuse was resented or satirised, not the institution. In the worst times of the Power, during the residence at Avignon and the schism which preceded the Council of Constance, all Europe longed for an independent and single head for its religious system.

In the year 1305 a French pope was elected to the chair. He almost immediately took up his residence at Avignon, where he and his successors remained for seventy years. All the popes who sat at Avignon were Frenchmen, and were supposed, perhaps with justice, to be devoted to French interests. Now, during the greater part of this time, England, or rather the English monarch, was at war with France. The successes of Edward and his warlike son made the war popular, in course of time. The reverses which overtook that monarch at the close of his reign were ascribed, in part at least, to the machinations of the French popes. The origin of those sentiments, which finally brought about a rupture between England and Rome, is a tradition derived from the jealousies which sprung out of the residence at Avignon, and the partial policy of the papal court. It had ceased to be international, it had voluntarily made itself the political thrall of the English enemy, and men became familiar with antipathy to an institution which might be perverted to interested or unjust ends.

While this unpopularity was growing, Europe was visited by a prodigious calamity—a calamity which has induced more lasting effects on the world than any other event of the kind, which effected a social revolution, and gave occasion to that peculiar developement of political and theological speculation which is connected with the names of Wiklif, of his disciples, and of his successors. It awakened an impulse towards discussing the theory of civil government, because it convulsed society. It provoked religious speculation, because the central religious authority having been, in this island at least, discredited, innovations in doctrine became familiar, and were for a time permitted, as they naturally sprung from hostility to the partisan pope.

Towards the latter half of the fourteenth century a new disease of astonishing deadliness invaded Eastern Europe. Like every other pestilence which has attacked mankind, it commenced in Central Asia, and travelled slowly westwards. Like every pestilence, it was infinitely more destructive at its first appearance than it has been since, for it still exists, under the name of the Plague. Its victims generally perished, sometimes perished suddenly. The symptoms of the disease were as appalling as they were intractable. The English people called it the Black Death.

It is said that half the population of Europe perished by the ravages of this terrible disease. Fear always exaggerates numbers; but it is certain that the mortality was enormous. The habits of our ancestors, five centuries ago, were not favourable to health. Their houses were squalid. Two centuries after the plague first appeared, the Spanish envoy of Philip II said, 'These English live like pigs; though,' he added, 'they fare as well as the king.' Hence the plague raged most fatally among the poorer classes, especially in the towns. The minds of men were so powerfully affected by this visitation, that the few philosophers of that age who tried to find a physical cause for the disease, saw or seemed to see and perceive a black fetid mist constantly rolling onwards from the desolated East.

No one can do more than guess at the loss which population sustained. For about thirty years before the coming of the Black Death, England had been nearly uniformly blessed with singularly prosperous seasons. Beyond doubt, as always happens under similar circumstances, the number of the people rapidly increased, for the growth of population as a continuous quantity depends upon the success with which agriculture is practised. Now a series of propitious seasons is equivalent to increased fertility.

Within a year or two after the plague began, the wages of common labour were doubled. In the face of such a sudden rise, the profitable employment of capital was annihilated. The feudal lord, who up to this time had cultivated his own land with the assistance of a bailiff, was unable to contend against this increase in the cost of the labour which he needed for his farming operations. In vain did these landowners attempt, as landowners have attempted once and again, to set up parliamentary enactments as a counter force to natural laws. In vain did the legislature strive to give effect to petitions for the relief of agricultural distress, i. e. landlords' distress, by attempting to fix the rate of wages. But the parliament of 1350 did more than commit a temporary error. It commenced that ruinous war between capital and labour, which has been carried on for more than five centuries; a war, the terms of whose cessation have not yet been announced by the numerous negotiators who have striven to deal with the quarrel and conclude it by a lasting peace.

The plague which devastated town and country was equally fatal in the monasteries and in the two universities. Before the great Death, it is said that Oxford contained 30,000 students. The number is, no doubt, an exaggeration; but it should be remembered that in those days the English universities were the great public schools of England, that there was far more familiar intercourse between the students of European nations than there is now, and that Oxford at least was in the zenith of her reputation at the time. The rivalry of religious orders was stereotyped in the system of their several philosophies. These rivalries extended to universities. Paris had endorsed the scholasticism of the Dominicans; Oxford had adopted that of the Franciscans. The former was the head-quarters of the Thomists, the latter of the Scotists. Almost at the very time of the calamity to which I am referring, the university of Prague was founded in imitation of Paris, Vienna in that of Oxford. In order to gain such literary reputation as the age acknowledged or rewarded, it was necessary for the student to repair to some university, and that of Oxford was eminently popular. Many of the great monasteries had their college or hall, to which they regularly sent some of their younger monks, in order that they might study and graduate.

In those days, the university of Oxford had, as it still has, an independent jurisdiction over its members. It had, in common with similar incorporations, obtained a grant of municipal privileges. In consequence of certain conflicts, sometimes prolonged, and always sanguinary, between the citizen and the students, the privileges of the town were subjected to those of the academical authorities, and the mayor was constrained, before he entered on his office, to swear fealty and obedience to the chancellor or chief officer of the university, who was elected biennially, as the rectors of the Scotch universities still are, by the suffrages of his academical subjects. To exercise an effectual discipline over these numerous students, no residence of such students was allowed, except in licensed houses, and under an acknowledged and elected superior. Such a house, once appropriated to academical, could not revert to secular uses. But so numerously did students throng to the medieval university, that the owners of house property constantly dedicated their tenements to the reception of these visitors, because they found it the most advantageous means of letting their estate.

The students either lived on their own resources, or were selected from the monastic novices, or, in rare cases, were maintained by benefactions held in trust by the university, or, still more rarely, in independent foundations, the members of which were constituted as a chartered corporation. Five of these foundations pretend to an antiquity before that of the great social convulsion to which I have referred; but of these, four were inchoate, and only one was really a collegiate establishment. There was as keen an ambition in those days among the small proprietors to send one of their sons to the university, as there is now in Ireland to equip a boy at Maynooth. Those who held by villain tenure were as ambitious as their neighbours. The lord guarded against the diminution of labourers on his estate, by checking migration from it; attempted to secure and enlarge his right over the inferior tenant, by exacting a fine on the departure of any male from the manor. If a man became a monk or priest, he was no longer a serf. Hence the manorial and bailiffs' accounts of the Middle Ages contain numerous entries of fines paid for licence to become a monk, or to enter at the public schools.

The beginning of the university of Oxford is lost in obscurity. The notices given of it in annals, written long before any college was founded, represent it as a vigorous and thriving institution, which had already attracted the notice and secured the patronage of popes and kings. A little after the middle of the thirteenth century, however, an English statesman, Walter Merton, who had secured the good-will of both parties during the Barons' War, resolved on founding an institution in Oxford, from which all monks should be rigidly excluded. This was the first Oxford college. It was richly endowed from its commencement, and soon became famous. The fundamental principle which it contained stereotyped, so to speak, that hostility between the secular students and the monastic orders which continued till the monastic system was finally suppressed. Oxford owed much of its learning and activity to the rivalry between these two powers.

All writers agree that the effect which the Black Death induced on the learning and the morals of the people was eminently disastrous. People often think that times of great and general distress are favourable to a reformation in morals and religion. Exactly the reverse is the truth, unless one confounds superstition with religion. It has been noted over and over again that a period of great mortality, of sudden misery, is often accompanied, generally followed, by dissoluteness. The ancient historian of Greece bears testimony to the fact that the Athenian plague was followed by deep political and social depravity. The same statement is made by the Italian writers, such as Boccacio, who were contemporary with the Black Death. So also speak the English annalists. There was no lack of profligacy and debauchery in the days of Charles the Second, after the last fearful visitation of the same calamity in 1662. The fact is, the fear of death does not deter from vice, so much as the sudden prospect of enjoyment provokes vice. Men who had been poor were suddenly enriched. The clergy had fallen victims to the plague in great numbers, and men pressed into the vast prizes which this profession offered at such a crisis. There is no better proof that a Church is depraved than the fact that the younger sons of an aristocracy grasp at and secure its emoluments by virtue of their birth. At the conclusion of the fourteenth century, this phenomenon was manifest enough. So it was in the worst ages of the Gallican Church. It should be noted that this general depravity was coupled with an ostentatious profession of orthodoxy, and a savage spirit of persecution. We owe the fires of Smithfield to these aristocratic prelates. Their support of the first king of the house of Lancaster was purchased with the passage of the statute for burning heretics. It is not in our own days only that a usurper seeks to enslave his subjects by enlisting the material interests of a hierarchy on his side.

It is essential, in order to understand the part which Wiklif played in the fourteenth century, and to explain the influence which his teaching had, that we should see the social state of England during that epoch. Power, as I have said, was very widely distributed, but the limits of every power were very loosely defined. The prerogatives of the monarch, the noble, the bishop, the lord of the manor-court, and, outside all, the pope, were uncertain. Interests clashed in all directions. Privileges were asserted, conceded, restrained, as circumstances gave a temporary opportunity to each. In one year, the pope is prohibited from granting English benefices to foreigners ; in the next, the statute is rescinded or suspended. One year, the king shows favour to the Lollards ; a year or two afterwards, he expels them from the universities. At one time, the Commons exhort the king to put the charges of the public revenue on the lands of the Church ; a short time elapses, and the same Commons pass a law under which the advocates of disendowment are burnt alive. One year, the king is controlled by a council, and is threatened with deposition ; a little while, and the same monarch is absolute. No one can interpret the politics of the fourteenth century, except he realises the fact that this contest of interests was perpetually going on, and accounts for the rise and decline of each on a principle similar to that which is called natural selection. At the base of this social system, one power was growing steadily and silently. The agriculturist was being gradually transformed from a serf or a tenant at a perpetual rack-rent, into that prosperous and independent yeoman who formed the back-bone of English society for many centuries. Upon this ferment of rival interests came the tremendous convulsion of the Great Plague.

A general tradition sets Wiklif's birth in the year 1324; but there are no positive grounds on which the tradition is supported. More solid evidence is given for the place of his birth, a village in Yorkshire some twelve miles north of Richmond, from which his name is derived. According to Dr. Vaughan, Wiklif's relations resided in the manor-house of this village till 1606, when the estate was carried by marriage into the family of the Tonstalls.

It is reported that he studied at Queen's College, Oxford; but this is, I think, unlikely, as this college was not founded till 1340, when Wiklif, the year of whose birth is certainly not antedated, would have been sixteen years old at least. It is most likely that he was on no foundation at first, and that subsequently he belonged to Merton College, which claims him as a fellow. This claim is neither modern nor dubious, for a list of all the fellows of this college since the foundation was drawn up in the first year of Henry the Sixth, thirty-eight years after Wiklif's death. In this list the reformer's name is specified. The number of fellows given in this list is nearly five hundred, but to Wiklif's name alone is annexed the date of his election, 1357. In the first year of Henry the Sixth, when John of Bedford was in power, when Wiklif's followers were proscribed, when it was felony to keep his books, when a bishop of Lincoln, in whose diocese Oxford then was, was in course of founding a college 'to write, preach, and dispute against the damnable doctrine of the Wiklevists,' the fellows of another Oxford college were not likely, without solid grounds of fact, to allow so detested a comrade of their society.

There is similar proof that he was Master of Balliol College in 1361. In the same year he was appointed rector of Fillingham in Lincolnshire, a benefice which had been at or about that time given to Balliol College by a clergyman named Cave. He had ceased to be Master of Balliol before 1365. In 1368 he exchanged his living for that of Ludgershall in Bucks, and in 1374, the latter for Lutterworth, a charge which he retained till his death. This occurred on Dec. 31, 1384. He was nominated to the last living by the king, for reasons which I shall state farther on.

I shall not attempt to give even a sketch of Wiklif's theological opinions, nor indeed allude to them, except where they seem to throw light on the position which he occupied as a social reformer and a politician. It was when the very fabric of this country was well nigh shattered to pieces by the insurrection of the boors in 1381, after all hopes of averting political reforms were frustrated by the reckless administration of the king's uncles, and the reformer was abandoned by his allies, that Wiklif withdrew from his political and social projects, and betook himself to speculative theology. His critical work on pure theology was published in that summer when Tyler and his associates almost effected a revolution. It was after this time that his theological enemies heaped adjectives and substantives on his head. One, Walsingham, after ransacking the copious vocabulary of monastic abuse, puns on his name. 'This Wikleve, or, to be more correct, Wicked beleve.' These substantives and adjectives increased in number and ferocity up to the Reformation. His contemporaries, while they abjured the heretic, spoke admiringly and even kindly of the man. Later on, he is the teacher of the Hussites, Polydore Vergil affirming even that he preached in Bohemia. Later still, he is 'the devil's standard-bearer, and the perpetual fuel of hell.' But in the first instance, as has been recognised by his biographers, the hostility which he provoked was chiefly political. It does not follow that this provocation was slight, if, as is constantly said, he asserted that the civil authority of the magistrate should override clerical pretensions. But his immediate foes were the monks and the friars.

The active life of a medieval chieftain was spent, as a rule, in wronging his neighbours. The shape which the penitence of his declining years and enfeebled powers took was that of benefiting the Church. Sometimes the reformed soldier or brigand became a monk, and as such was famous for his humility, or his austerities, or his enthusiasm. So in the worst ages of modern society, the noisiest and most frivolous profligates have often become the most rigid and mortified Trappists or Carthusians. It may be doubted whether Churches have been wise when they have gloried in such portentous conversions.

For several centuries the ecclesiastics throve on these devotees. Many writers have commented on the profusion with which the Anglo-Saxon kings and thanes endowed their monks. The Norman and Plantagenet monarchs put checks on the practice, more, it seems, because such a dedication debarred the superior lord from enjoying the dues which were levied on successions, and the waste which could be committed during a tenant's minority, than from any subtler motives of public policy. Now it was reckoned that at the end of the fourteenth century the Church held half the land in the country, and that land not the least fertile. Had these riches been spent in a popular manner, perhaps the possession would not have been grudged; but the habits of prelate and abbot were those of the great lords around them— ostentatious, luxurious, and in many cases profligate.

In order to counteract the vices of the older and

richer orders, Francis and Dominic founded their fraternities of begging friars. These monks were prohibited from acquiring any permanent possessions. Even the monasteries occupied by them were not their own, but were held in trust for them, generally by the town corporations in whose vicinity they ordinarily took up their abode. They tended the sick, especially those whom others neglected and loathed, for in those days leprosy in its worst Eastern form was frightfully common; they became the favourite confessors of the wealthy, from whose penitence they could make no gain; and they formed a body of local preachers, if I may be allowed to use a modern equivalent for their functions, whose homely and earnest discourses were peculiarly acceptable to the people among whom they ministered. In time, however, the same occurrence which induced so general a depravity in society, affected the character, and with it the reputation, of the Minorite Friars. It is hardly possible to keep an endowed Church pure, an endowed institution useful.

The secular students in the University of Oxford had a standing feud with the religious orders. It seems that monks were not easily admitted to degrees in Arts. It was debated whether they should be allowed to graduate in Divinity. The faculty which they generally professed was Law, and the University discouraged this degree, by curtailing it of the privileges which it bestowed on that of Masters of Arts. I have seen a sermon of the fifteenth century, in which the preacher argues that both Scripture and reason confer the functions of academical government on Masters and on Masters only. His argument is, 'Ye call Me Master and Lord.'

The universities prided themselves on their independence. When Gregory XI despatched his bull to Oxford, commanding the chancellor to send Wiklif to London, that he might be tried for his opinions, this interference with the privilege of the University was emphatically resented. When, again, only three years before Wiklif's death, the Archbishop of Canterbury required the University to issue a formal condemnation of his tenets, he having then thrown down the gauntlet by publishing an attack on the doctrine of transubstantiation, the University, at its annual election of magistrates, returned Wiklif's friends to office, and submitted only to a mandate of the king, and a threat that its franchises should be revoked, if it continued refractory. Nor after Wiklif's death, and when the persecution was raised against his sectaries, did the University forget the representative of its independence, for the chancellor who resisted the archbishop's mandate in 1382 was re-elected to the same office in 1386. 'No bishop or archbishop,' said this bold chancellor, Dr. Robert Rugge, 'has any authority whatsoever over the University in matters of belief.' Of this again.

Oxford, then, was a refuge for speculative opinion at a time when novelties in belief were peculiarly dangerous to the person who was reported to entertain them. During the epoch of this independence, it was great and powerful. It declined in vigour and reputation immediately on its subjection to ecclesiastical control, in the days of Elizabeth. Its influence as a social power was utterly extinguished when it was constrained to submit to the legislation of Laud, and was subsequently bound by the Act of Uniformity.

It is not difficult to discover the causes of Wiklif's early popularity within and without his University. He was, according to the learning of the age, singularly learned. He erred, says an unfriendly annalist (and all the annalists are unfriendly to him), through the subtlety and profundity of his mind, through his incomparable learning. His simplicity, gentleness, gravity, and earnestness are similarly witnessed to. But besides, he was intensely national. His first quarrel with the pope was provoked by what he held to be the presumptuous arrogance of the pontiff. He despised the favours and ridiculed the threats of the Roman see. He argued that all ecclesiastics should be subject to the civil power. The essence of his ecclesiastical system was political utility. He made no distinction, says Melancthon, in exaggeration, between the gospel and the state. It was on principles like these that he argued, when the king consulted him as to whether he might conscientiously forbid, in a time of great financial distress, the transmission of any contribution to the papal coffers, that such an act was not only justifiable, but a public duty.

He detested the friars, quite as much because they were the emissaries and adherents of the pope, as he did for academical or theological reasons. They were to him the representatives of a foreign system which claimed the spiritual allegiance of Englishmen, but which abused that allegiance in order to strengthen the hands of England's hereditary enemy, and which fleeced the native clergy in order to subsidise a horde of needy and treacherous foreigners. It may be, as some modern apologists have alleged, that the Avignon popes were as honest arbiters in Christian politics as any of their predecessors or successors. But no Englishman of the fourteenth century entertained this impression. Nay, had Europe been generally of that mind, the gathering at Constance, which decreed that a general council was superior to the pope, and thereupon asserted one of Wiklif's favourite maxims, that the pope was neither paramount, nor irresponsible nor infallible, would never have met. It has been observed that Wiklif's influence declined after the return of the popes to Rome, even though the schism took place almost immediately on the return. But Urban, who prosecuted Wiklif, was acknowledged by England, and favoured the English policy.

This keen spirit of nationality gives, I repeat, the key to Wiklif's influence at Edward's court. It accounts perhaps for the fact, that when he attempted to substitute for the Minorite Friars a body of wandering preachers whom he called his 'simple priests,' the bishops, who had not been as energetically attacked by him as the monastic orders were, licensed and encouraged these missionaries. It explains his great and enduring popularity at the universities, where his followers flourished long after they were elsewhere proscribed. He was no doubt disliked by what may be called the Conservative statesmen of the time, such as Wykeham and Courtenay; but had his innovating tendencies been confined to social reforms, he might perhaps have retained his influence in public affairs, and might even, as Dr. Shirley suggests, have founded a religious order of a purely national character.

In 1369, Charles V of France broke the treaty of Bretigny, and Edward resumed the title of king of France. It is not improbable that William de Grimoard de Beauvoir, lord of Grisac in Gévaudan, and abbot of S. Victor at Marseilles, whom the Papal fasti know as Urban V, may have counselled, or at least condoned, this breach of solemn oaths. Of course the war between the two countries was instantly renewed, and in 1371 two parliaments were summoned in order to make provision for the growing charges of the contest. At this period, the unpopularity of the Church was at its height. Wiklif appears to have been present at the debate which gave expression to this feeling. In the first of these assemblies the Commons granted a tax on each parish.

In those days statistics were not forthcoming, and the parliament guessed the English parishes at five times their actual number. But the nobles, it appears, looked angrily at the wealth of the monastic orders, and demanded that they should contribute handsomely to the charges of the State. Perhaps they thought them the allies or satellites of Urban. And then, adds Wiklif, a certain shrewd lord applied a fable to these monks. He said that on a time the birds were holding an assembly. There came among them an owl, featherless and wretched. He begged a feather from each bird present. In compassion they helped him to a plumage. Suddenly the owl turns to a hawk, and begins to make havoc among his benefactors. Upon this, they bethought themselves, each to demand back the feathers which he had given, and of which so ill a use had been made. In the end, said he, the owl was more bare and forlorn than when he came to beg at first. So, he added, we must treat these monks. They are tricked out in our feathers, they mock us with their abundance, and our wisdom is to make them bare again. There were twenty-six abbots and priors present at this apologue. The bishops, whose jurisdiction over the monks was generally superseded by the pope, were not perhaps so much offended.

The clergy met the crisis by a liberal subsidy, for they granted as large an aid as that which parliament gave. But in the summer session of the same year, the parliament petitions the king, that henceforth eminent offices of state should not be occupied by clergymen, specifying as offices those of chancellor, treasurer, clerk of the privy seal, barons of the exchequer, comptrollers, and other great officers and governors. The king declined to grant this petition formally, though the Commons aver that great mischief and damage has been done by these means. But he acted on the hint. He displaced William of Wykeham from the office of chancellor, and the Bishop of Exeter from that of treasurer, putting into their places Sir Robert Thorp, a judge, and Lord Scroop of Bolton, two laymen. The same parliament corrected the statistical error which had been made in the spring.

In the following year the Earl of Pembroke was sent to Guienne, in order to relieve Rochelle. The Spaniards had been made enemies to the English by the Black Prince's unlucky advocacy of Peter the Cruel, and by the marriage of the prince's brothers with the two daughters of Peter, and the consequent claims of John of Gaunt to the crown of Castile. John of Gaunt, Duke of Lancaster, did not, it is true, occupy an inch of Spanish soil; but the experience of his father's wars with France had made even a title dangerous, and Henry of Castile, who had the memories of Najara before him, saw that it was wise to link his cause with that of the French king. So he sent a fleet to Rochelle, which surprised the English ships and totally destroyed them on the 23rd of June. The military chest of the English force was captured, and the Earl of Pembroke and his companies were taken prisoners. 'His fate,' says the chronicler who continues the history of Adam of Monmouth, 'was to be expected. He was the fierce enemy of the ecclesiastics in the previous parliament, for he advised the king and his council to demand great subsidies from the clergy, and to insist that in time of war their contributions should be heavier than those of the laity. The precedent of the parliament of 1371 was followed, the Church was burdened with exactions, and the world at large saw the judgment on these deeds.' Considering that the wealth of the clergy was prodigious, and that the source of this wealth was tithes and rents, which were taxed on their annual value only, while the subsidies of the people were a certain quota of their capital, levied in the form of a property tax, and amounting often to a fifteenth or twentieth of their personal estate, it is not perhaps strange that the laity clamoured for a more equitable adjustment of public burdens, that the nobles advised the king to demand a portion of these resources, and that the monks were constrained to find their consolation in believing that the vengeance of Heaven fell on those who made Church lands contribute in a somewhat fairer measure to the exigencies of the government. Edward, who tried to relieve Rochelle in August, was detained by contrary winds.

The papal court had long claimed the right of

anticipating the presentation to vacant benefices by granting in certain cases to those clergymen whom it favoured, or who found the means to purchase such a privilege, the expectation of ecclesiastical emoluments. Such a usurpation on the rights of patrons was naturally resented and resisted. Originally, perhaps, the practice was defended by ecclesiastics, in order to protect the Church against royal or aristocratical rapacity, and formed part of that scheme for maintaining the balance of political and social forces which constituted in the action of the papacy the equivalent for what we should now call Public Opinion. Frequently, too, the monarch recognised this dangerous prerogative of the pope, in order that he might provide for his own clerical dependants at the expense of the private rights of ecclesiastical patrons. But the custom had long outgrown these beginnings. The popes made the sale of these Provisions (as the grant of such reversions was called) a means for replenishing their exchequer, and both king, nobles, and clergy loudly demanded that a stop should be put to the practice.

The remedy was supplied by a statute enacted in 1350, and known to constitutional lawyers under the name of 'The Statute of Provisors.' It declared that the court of Rome should not collate to any bishopric or living in England; and that if any person disturbed any patron in the presentation of a living, by virtue of such an instrument from the pope, such a person should pay fine and ransom to the king, and be imprisoned till he renounced his pretended right. This act was subsequently held to bring the offender within the penalties of a præmunire, i.e. the liability to forfeit lands and goods, to be outlawed, and thereupon put out of the right of prosecuting any personal injury which any person might inflict on the culprit: a rule promulgated with tremendous effect in the days of Henry VIII. The remedy was sharp enough, but so weak was the executive, or so terrible to the minds of the faithful was still the risk of disobeying the commands of the pope, that the practice of making these Provisions was continued, notwithstanding the statute. As might be expected, Wiklif was a strenuous opponent of this usurpation, and advocated its peremptory cessation.

Towards the latter end of his reign, Edward the Third entered into negotiations with the pope (Gregory XI) with a view to effecting a compromise. The Statute of Provisors was apparently very indifferently observed, for in 1373, when these negotiations were commenced, three English prelates died, viz. the Archbishop of York and the Bishops of Ely and Worcester. Their successors were forthwith appointed by the pope. Two of them, it is true, were scions of noble English families, Nevil and Arundel. But the first embassy appears to have been a failure.

On March 9, 1374, Edward returned to the attack. He wrote a very courteous letter to Gregory, informing him that it is necessary to take certain steps in order to meet the inconvenience and scandal of the present practice, and telling him that he intends to send certain ambassadors to Bruges, with a view to laying the facts before him or his representative. He begs that during the interval all causes commenced in the pope's court should be suspended, in as full a manner as causes would be suspended in the king's courts, whenever a question might arise as to the power of the court to adjudicate on the matter laid before it. Nor does he confine himself to remonstrance. On May 3, a writ is directed to the sheriff of Wilts, commanding him to stop all bulls, processes, letters, and the like, emanating from the Roman see, and affecting the rights of persons in England. This writ is probably the specimen of a class.

On July 26 the commission of the ambassadors was issued. It constituted John, bishop of Bangor, John de Wiklif, professor of theology, John Gates, dean of Segovia, Simon de Multon, doctor of laws, William de Burton, Robert de Belknap, and John de Hanynton, a commission of embassy. Five of them (always including the Bishop of Bangor) were to constitute a quorum, who should treat with the pope on the subject of Provisions.

These men seem to have debated and fully agreed on terms with the pope. On the 1st of September, 1375, an elaborate document was issued from the Roman court, conceding all that the king required, and abandoning the usurpation which had been so long exercised. The king, for his part, surrendered the use of a writ, by which he assumed the right to confer benefices, under certain circumstances. Edward rewarded his ambassadors—at least three of them, for he made Belknap Chief Justice of the King's Bench, translated the Bishop of Bangor to the see of Hereford, and gave the living of Lutterworth to Wiklif. On Wiklif's return to England, he appears to have resided for some time at Oxford, for he rents rooms in Queen's College during parts of the year 1374-75. It must have been during this time that he extended his reputation as a preacher and a politician.

In 1376, the Commons took certain energetic steps, in order to effect the reformation of abuses. It is supposed that the Prince of Wales was jealous of the Duke of Lancaster and his followers, and that he instigated the opposition to the king and to those who acted in his name. Edward was now old and feeble both in mind and body, and was supposed to be under the influence of the duke, of Lord Latimer, and of one Alice Perrers, whom parliament boldly charged with various impudent malpractices. For a time a reform was effected. But the prince died, the duke and his associates were reinstated, and the Speaker of the House of Commons, Peter de la Mare, expiated his attack on the court and the lady by a two years' imprisonment in Nottingham gaol. This parliament was long known in history by the epithet of 'the good,' but its influence was, it is plain, exceedingly transient, though it supplied a precedent in time to come for parliamentary impeachment.

The boldness of Wiklif's speculations on political and ecclesiastical subjects was now commanding attention. Attracted by his eloquence and humour, by the novelty of his opinions, and by the courage with which he avowed them, a number of persons became his disciples at Oxford. As I stated above, the principal objects of his hostility were the various monastic orders, and especially the begging friars. These men had no country, no sense of public duty; they were the mere creatures and spies of the pope, according to Wiklif. But the reformer attacked the ecclesiastical relations of the friars only, not the mortified life which they professed but did not practise. He proposed to substitute for them a body of poor preaching priests, who should go about the country and rouse men to faith and good works. So he gathered about himself a number of followers, dressed in russet,—that is, in unbleached and undyed cloth,—barefoot, and bound to wander about and preach. His theory of a reform was a revival, but a revival accompanied by the machinery which should make the religious awakening a permanent feeling.

The real object of Wiklif's attack was the existing ecclesiastical system. The Roman Church, he argued, is no more the head of all Churches than any other. St. Peter was not more gifted than any other apostle. The pope has no higher spiritual power than any other ordained minister. The State can disendow a delinquent Church, and ought to do so. The rules of the monastic orders add no more intrinsic holiness to the profession of the monks than whitewash does solidity to a wall. Neither pope nor bishop should imprison men for conscience' sake. The excessive wealth of the clergy should be reduced. Nor did Wiklif neglect to use his wit against the objects of his hate. When one of his followers said that Scripture did not recognise the friars, 'It does,' said Wiklif, 'in the text, I know you not.'

Wiklif's opinions gained him admirers among the nobles. When, therefore, he appeared in 1377 before the Convocation assembled in London, in order to defend himself against the charges laid on him, he came under the protection of the Duke of Lancaster and the Earl Marshal. The bishop bade him stand, the duke told him to sit. The bishop said he was in the position of a criminal before his judges. The duke insisted that he was there to argue about his opinions, and to argue freely. The altercation grew so fierce, that duke and earl insulted the bishop, and broke up the sitting. The Londoners, we are told, sided with the bishop, and, taking up arms, strove to kill the duke, and were dissuaded only by the bishop's earnest exhortation from burning his house in the Savoy. The duke was at this time excessively unpopular. But John of Gaunt was not a man to be easily browbeaten. He had left London, and was at Kingston. But he forthwith returned, and ejecting the mayor and aldermen from their offices, set up others in their room. The new mayor was Richard Whittington.

It was not likely that the bishops would allow themselves to be baffled. They forthwith appealed to the pope. The first meeting had been held on Feb. 23. The bulls, dated May 31, arrived in London in October, and were addressed to the Archbishop of Canterbury, the Bishop of London, the King, and the University of Oxford. In the interval Edward had died, and Richard, assisted by a regency of twelve persons, was on the throne. The bulls condemned certain propositions ascribed to Wiklif. The University was beyond measure indignant at this interference with its fundamental privilege of exercising its own jurisdiction over its own members in matters of faith as well as in moral discipline. Wiklif, however, came to London. But Joan, Richard's mother, who favoured the opinions of Wiklif, interposed, and forbad further action, sending her orders by Sir Louis Clifford. The mob, now on Wiklif's side, broke in and dispersed the conclave. The sympathy which the princess felt towards Wiklif was subsequently shared by Anne of Bohemia, Richard's queen. Shortly afterwards Gregory died, the great schism in the papacy began, and Wiklif had some breathing-time. He now redoubled his efforts, and sought to organise his reforms. He came forward, however, to defend his patron, the Duke of Lancaster, against an act, perpetrated by the duke's adherents or dependants, and in his interest. This act, if it be told fairly, needed every defence possible.

Two esquires, Hawley and Shakel, had taken prisoner the Count of Denia, a Spanish nobleman. The count, on leaving his son as a hostage for his father's ransom, had been released and had returned to Spain. The young man, now in the hands of his father's captors, was, it appears, an important captive in the eyes of John of Gaunt, who still laid claim to the crown of Castile. By the custom of war,—the relics of the custom remain to our day in the rules which regulate the distribution of prize money,—the ransom of the prisoner was the property of his captors. John of Gaunt, wishing to obtain possession of the young man, offered to purchase him from the esquires. It seems that they refused to treat with the duke and king.

Upon this John of Gaunt procured an act of parliament, under which Hawley and Shakel were sent to the Tower. It is not easy to discover the plea on which such an act was obtained, if indeed the story is told correctly by the chronicler. Wiklif's defence of the prince seems to be that the esquires were guilty of treason in declining to treat with the titular king of Castile, and in having broken from the Tower. But it is not easy to see how the imputation of an offence against the king of Castile could be treason against the dignity of an English monarch; and it is still more difficult to find how an escape from prison could be construed as treason. Yet it was harder to justify, even in that age and apart from the circumstances which followed the imprisonment of the esquires, the subsequent act of Lancaster's adherents.

The count had been liberated on parol by his captors, and had gone into concealment. After some time the esquires escaped from the Tower, and took refuge in the sanctuary at Westminster, apparently within the abbey church itself. Here, on August 11, 1378, and in the middle of high mass, when the privilege of sanctuary was at the highest, Ralph de Ferrers, one of the duke's dependants, broke into the church with forty armed followers, murdered Hawley, and capturing Shakel, took him back to prison. To the habits of the time, it was impossible to conceive any act more unknightly, more unchristian, more illegal. I state the adjectives in the order according to which public opinion in that time arranged them. The modern gentleman transposes the last two.

The right of sanctuary, which was afterwards so grossly abused, was in rude days a real refuge against atrocious oppression. Even in minor matters it was a protest against the summary jurisdiction of the time. To violate it was, therefore, accounted a crime of no common atrocity, and was certain to incur the strongest ecclesiastical censures. The offence was gross in this case, and no doubt the better part of public opinion went with them when the Archbishop of Canterbury, the Bishop of London, and the other suffragans of Canterbury excommunicated the actors of this crime and their abettors.

The temper of the Plantagenet princes was rough. Princes are seldom gentle when crossed, and John of Lancaster, a hot-tempered prince at all times, and now a titular king, was furious. He could not treat the London citizens and their bishop (who seems to have been popular, and who would have been, under any circumstances, popular in supporting or defending the right of Sanctuary) as his brother had treated Limoges. He gathered a parliament at Gloucester (the king was twelve years old), and strove to give effect to the extremest doctrines of the reformers. His scheme would have annihilated the power of the clergy as completely as that of Cromwell, and Cranmer, and Henry the Eighth did a century and a half later, when the leaven of Lollardism had penetrated the people. But John was foiled, as far as regarded vengeance, and had to be satisfied with impunity.

Wiklif offered a defence, which, I think, is little creditable to him, except on the ground that he was bound to support a valuable ally, who seemed to sustain a good cause, as the Puritans supported Leicester under similar circumstances. He admits the right of sanctuary under certain conditions; hints that the esquires had been guilty of high treason constructively; and says that they had been offered 1000*l.*—a vast sum then—to let the prisoner escape.

It appears from Dr. Shirley's researches that Wiklif was still occupying rooms in Queen's College during the year 1380. From certain facts which may be found in the 'Foedera,' Queen's College—founded, it seems, for the purpose of being a seminary in which young men of noble family might be instructed—was suspected of Lollardism, or at least of insubordination. In the winter of that year he was seriously ill. During his sickness, and when it seemed dangerous, we are told that certain friars, attended by some citizens who sided with them, got admission to Wiklif's rooms, as he lay in bed, worn out, and half unconscious. The friars, after expressing their good wishes for his recovery, presumed the other alternative, and then adjured him, before such a contingency could happen, to express his regret that he had assailed them so fiercely. Wiklif, always wan, and now wasted with sickness, bade his attendants lift him up, and then, let us hope with a true sense of the humour of his reply, said, 'I shall not die, but live, and recount the evil deeds of the friars.'

It is plain that Lancaster claimed the young count as a traitor to him and his Castilian crown, and we may concede that Wiklif defended his protector from a sense of gratitude, and on the plea of policy. The protection was reckoned valuable. Knighton, a contemporary of Wiklif, says, that 'had it not been for Lancaster, Wiklif and his associates would have fallen with contempt into the pit of destruction.'

The check given to the ecclesiastics in the two conclaves of 1377 must have been invaluable to the reformer, since he gained time in which to methodise his system and organise his following. It is impossible to estimate how strong that organisation would have been, if it had not been discredited by the tremendous insurrection of 1381, an event so vast and so unparalleled that I must needs speak at length on its circumstances, though I will seek to condense the facts into as narrow a compass as I can.

Under the social system of our ancestors, six centuries ago and onwards, land was the cheapest kind of property. The art of agriculture was so little developed that a fourfold return to seed was a good average. The farmer knew nothing of winter roots, of artificial grasses, and, except in its most rudimentary form, of the rotation of crops. As the produce was scanty, so the stock was poor. There was no selection of breeds, for all kinds were equally ill-fed and stunted, and consequently none of that competition of breeders with which we are now so familiar. But nearly the whole population was engaged in agriculture. It is said that the motive of the long vacation at the law courts and the universities was to enable every person to assist in getting in the harvest. Business and study were therefore suspended from the beginning of July to the middle of October. The best arable land was let at sixpence an acre in money of the time; land which now lets for fifty shillings. You will understand the growth of productiveness in England, when I state that while corn has risen in price about nine times over that which formed an average five or six centuries ago, the rent of land has risen a hundred times. The rise and growth of rent are the result of prodigious improvements in the art of agriculture.

Everybody possessed land, though he invariably paid rent or some equivalent for it; the noble to the king, the peasant to his lord. The only exceptions to this universal obligation were the Church and the monasteries, who were supposed to render an equivalent for their possessions in prayers and other offices. In course of time, the nobles and freeholders achieved, through the great Charter and subsequent statutes, the right of assessing some of their obligations to the king at their discretion, of withholding or conceding a grant at their pleasure. But they did not surrender the right of taxing their own dependants.

There was no real slavery. But there was a class of occupying tenants who were not, it seems, liable to sudden eviction, or to the confiscation of their property, but who are called serfs, villains, or boors. These occupiers were bound to do certain services to their lords, these services, though predial, and called base, being fixed in quantity, and exactly similar to some of the Irish labour-rents. Now, as I said above, land was the cheapest object of value. It is now known that forced labour is seldom worth much, and that a labour-rent does not differ materially from forced labour. When the land reforms in Prussia were being carried out, it was found that the same fact held good in that country, and that a commutation of labour-rents was in the highest degree expedient to the landowner. So the landowner in medieval England was glad to commute his labour-rent for a money payment, and it is clear that such a conversion had been going on rapidly in England during the first half of the fourteenth century.

Then came, like a hurricane, the terrible visitation of the Great Plague. The price of common labour instantly doubled, and the landowner could no more cultivate his large farm at a profit. I have seen and examined many landlords' accounts of the time I refer to, and find that while, before this visitation, the profits of an owner who farmed his own land were, deducting rent, as high as eighteen per cent., the rate of profit after the plague instantly sunk to three per cent. It was impossible to carry on farming on such disadvantageous terms.

It was now found that the money commutation of labour-rents was disastrous to the landowner. The labour was worth double the amount of the commutation. An attempt was therefore made to recover part of the loss by a revision of these bargains, or, to put ancient facts into modern phrases, to tamper with tenant-right. In some instances, no doubt, the attempt succeeded. But whatever the measure of success was, it is certain that the attempt caused universal disaffection.

That the disaffection was fomented by the preaching of Wiklif's disciples cannot be doubted. The sermons of his principal followers are full of social allusions, and no one ever challenges one social practice without implying the discussion of all social practices. 'Christ,' said Nicholas Hereford, in his discourses, 'never bade any one beg. No one ought to give alms to a man whose clothes are better than his own. The civil law forbids able-bodied men to beg, and the gospel does not command it.' John de Aston charged the bishops with buying their sees, avowed that there would be no peace till ecclesiastics were deprived of their temporal possessions, said that if the king had the Church lands there would be no more need for taxes and tallages, and commented on the gratifying spectacle of a primitive bishop who, like St. Paul, worked with his own hands. Such sentiments were preached before the University, and we may be sure that plainer language was used to the rustics, the outlandish folk of the country.

Among these preachers none were more active than William Smith and William Swynderby. 'The former of these,' says an unfriendly annalist, 'was short and deformed. He had been passionately in love with a young woman, who rejected his suit. Forthwith he became an austere man, vowed a single life, left off linen; abjured flesh, fish, wine, and beer, as if they were poison; went about barefoot, and in middle age learned to read and write.' Among the exploits which are ascribed to him, was that of having lighted the fire in the lepers' chapel at Leicester with an image of St. Catherine. 'But then,' adds Walsingham, 'all the Lollards hated images; they even called the image of our Lady at Lincoln the Witch of Lincoln.' Smith was an indefatigable scribe, and busied himself incessantly in transcribing English books on religious subjects. The increased use of paper, the art of manufacturing which was perfected at about the middle of the fourteenth century, rendered this work comparatively easy. These books were valued as choice treasures, and when, a few years after, a fiery persecution fell on the Lollards, men were ready to give up their lives rather than surrender their books.

As William Smith went beyond the Oxford preachers, so William Swynderby went beyond Smith. He railed at the women for their extravagant dress, till they tried to stone him; he denounced the rich merchants and rich landlords, till he drove them to despair. He advised the people to withhold tithes and offerings from immoral and incompetent priests, and announced the Divine wrath against those who sued or imprisoned their debtors. He defied the censures of Buckingham, bishop of Lincoln. Seized and condemned by the bishop, he was begged off by the Duke of Lancaster. But he had to recant his errors in the three chief churches of Leicester, at Melton Mowbray, and at Loughborough. Subsequently he escaped from his prison and preached again at Coventry.

Other priests, such as were Ball and Straw, went still further. They preached about the natural equality of man, of the descent of all from a common and humble stock; of the profusion and rapacity of those who make themselves rich, and keep others poor by violence; of the hopelessness of attempting to better the condition of the peasantry, except by a combination and an uprising; of the necessity of meeting force by force, and of supplying funds for the purpose. For these preachings Ball was imprisoned in Maidstone gaol, whence he was released by Tyler's men. That the communications between the malcontent rustics were made by the wandering preachers, and that the moneys collected for the purposes of mutual defence were entrusted to the hands of the same persons, is either stated or implied by the contemporary chroniclers.

On the 10th of June, 1381, the storm, which no politician of the day appears to have anticipated, burst. The insurrection was simultaneous, in Kent and along the east coast as far as Scarborough. Norfolk, then the richest English county, fully shared in the rebellion, for the rioters took Norwich by storm. On the west it extended from Hants to Lancashire. The annals of the time give detailed accounts of the march of Tyler to London, the sack of the Tower, the murder of the archbishop, the audience between the king and Tyler at Mile-end and Blackheath, the murder of the latter by Walworth, and the collapse of the insurrection. But, except incidentally, we do not hear of the wide-spread character of the uprising.

We are told by Walsingham that Tyler was a man of great abilities. It is said that his ultimate purpose was to secure the king's person, and thus having obtained a semblance of authority, to use it for the purpose of destroying the feudal system, and of establishing in its room a government of counties or districts, the administration of which should be carried on by men of principles similar to his own. There is no inherent improbability in this story. It was the plan subsequently adopted by Cromwell. In any case it proves that Tyler was believed to be influenced by motives more extensive than the remedy of personal wrongs.

The king who had been forced to grant charters to the insurgents, revoked them when the danger was passed, under the advice and with the sanction of Parliament. The rolls of Parliament contain a long list of the ringleaders. In the county of Suffolk, three of them are described as beneficed clergymen. These people were tried and executed by a special commission; though after sufficient chastisement had been inflicted, a general pardon was issued, at the instance, said Richard, of Anne of Bohemia his espoused wife. But after all, the demands of the rioters were effectually conceded. The king uses indignant language towards the malcontents, Parliament emphatically refuses to recognise their claims, the successor of Simon Sudbury in the primacy speaks of them as shoeless ribalds, the warrior prelate of Norwich, Henry Spencer, attacked, defeated, judged, shrived and hanged them. But they got their demands; from villains they became prosperous and independent yeomen. Perhaps, in those days, statesmen such as the Earl of Salisbury and the Duke of Lancaster had learned that coercion never cures agrarian disaffection, and that it is impossible to subdue a whole people in order to satisfy a rapacious aristocracy, even one which had not yet been described as felonious.

Again, it is worth while to note, that disaffection, when it is based upon grounds which seem to be natural and just to those who entertain the feeling, is not checked by prosperity, but only by security. The insurrection of despair (such as that of the Jacquerie of France in 1358, and of the Irish periodically during the sixteenth, seventeenth, and eighteenth centuries), though accompanied by circumstances which are infinitely more appalling, is generally unfruitful. In every one of these cases, the insurgents were not only defeated, but, for a time at least, crushed into far greater helplessness and misery than before. The English insurgents of 1381 were, on the whole, prosperous. The country had been devastated by pestilence—that check to population which in medieval times fulfilled the function which wholesale emigration does in our day—and the survivors prospered. The last twenty-five years of the fourteenth century were years of plenty, and the farmer—that is the mass of the people—was thriving. It was because the boors of the fourteenth century were well-to-do folk, that they persevered in their efforts, and extorted the equitable right of the tenant against the legal right of the landlord, though from an unwilling and remonstrant aristocracy. While human nature remains the same, history is apt to reproduce itself. Of this at least I am persuaded, that when agrarian reforms are persistently demanded, they are, on due cause being shown, inevitably, even though slowly, conceded.

That Wiklif sympathised with the mass of the people is certain. Every religious reformer is driven, when he appeals to the reason, to enlist the sympathies of the people with him. Now Wiklif was eminently practical in his preaching, especially up to the time in which he was silenced at Oxford. He aimed at social reforms. It was because he thoroughly understood the forces which impeded these social reforms that he became an advocate of certain speculative opinions, which ran counter to the orthodoxy of the time. He attacked the pope and his emissaries, the wealthy and worldly abbots and bishops, and the whole political system of religion, before he assailed transubstantiation and sacerdotalism.

It was a favourite adage of Wiklif, that 'dominion is founded in grace.' This quaint theological expression, when interpreted in modern language, means no more than that obedience to government is based on its moral uses. To a government immoral, selfish, rapacious, Wiklif counselled resistance. But his resistance is endurance and remonstrance. 'Antichrist argues thus,' he says in one of his sermons, 'to keep men fighting, teaching that men should fight, as an adder naturally stings a man who treads on her. And why should we not fight against our enemies, else they would destroy us? But here methinks the fiend destroys many by the falseness of his reasons, and principles. If it be lawful to withstand violence by strength, it is lawful to fight with them that stand against us. Well I wot that angels stand against fiends, and many men by strength of law withstand their enemies and kill them not, nor even fight against them. But wise men of the world hold these means for strength, and thus vanquish their enemies without stroke; and men of the gospel vanquish by patience, and come to rest and peace by suffering. Right so we may do, if we keep charity.' In many particulars the leading Lollards were like the early Quakers. So, again, Wiklif understood the humanising effect of commerce, as well as the value of good government as a means of progress. 'So,' says he in one of his works, 'if this realm of England were ruled by reason, the thing that comes forth in the land would suffice it for meat and drink. But well I wot that God has ordained one land to be plenteous in one manner of thing, and one in another, for cause that they should come in charity. But this is much lost by wars and covetise.'

The legal fiction which makes a monarch sacred and his advisers responsible was unknown in Wiklif's day. But that a nation should reject an authority which was exercised to its own detriment was a received maxim in politics, and when Wiklif expressed this rule, in the formula stated above, he was merely reflecting back on the pope his own plea for interference in the state affairs of those countries which acknowledged his spiritual authority. In theory the pope was the keeper of dogmatic truth. But they who insist on orthodoxy invariably assert, as a safeguard to their claim, that laxity of belief is coupled with laxity of practice. To reverse this position, and say that laxity of practice is an index of laxity of belief, is natural, easy, and obvious. To extend the function of interference under this pretext, and to chastise delinquency as the outcome of a secret heresy, is sure to be the policy of ecclesiastical authority. And this is precisely what the popes did. They excused themselves for criticising the morals of kings and nobles on the ground that their acts caused scandal to the faith. Indeed, on the assumption that there should be such a thing as ecclesiastical discipline, I do not see how the inference can be avoided. Nothing but a political establishment will tolerate open and notorious profligacy in the nominal members of a Church, or insist that a man is entitled to all the privileges of Christianity who violates every one of its precepts.

But though the pope of the fourteenth century arrogated this authority over the lives and consciences of men, he claimed to be personally irresponsible. He affected to be a spiritual autocrat. The world had not yet prepared itself to hold that he was infallible. As yet this paradox was only a whim of the Dominican schoolmen, or a trick of canon lawyers, obscurely hinted at in the forged Decretals, and like our legal fiction that 'the king can do no wrong.' The followers of Buddha believe that in the uplands of Thibet there is a perpetual incarnation of the Deity, the discovery of which is vouchsafed to such favoured priests as can detect, by certain bodily marks, the indelible signs of the Divine presence in a child. But the Thibetan incarnation makes no revelation, is nothing but the silent centre of a contemplative, perhaps a negative, creed. There are, we are told, persons who assume a larger share of the Divine attributes to the Lama of the Western world. There are people who claim for an aged Italian priest, chosen by the intrigues of a restless and reactionary conclave, which protests against the laws of God in the natural world and has failed in every moral duty, the awful functions of revelation and prophecy.

The modern partisans of the Ultramontane school assert indeed that the Roman see has been the author or patron of all learning, knowledge, progress; has been the great and wise benefactor of the human race. The assertion is notoriously false; but this defence of the pope and his policy is a significant deference to the fact that no institution can claim the respect of men, unless it gives evidence of utility; that no ruler can claim authority over his fellow creatures as of right. 'It was something,' says Sismondi of those French nobles who entered into a League to withstand Louis XI, 'that these men acknowledged that there is a Public Good, however little their acts were in accordance with their admissions.'

In the summer of 1381, when he lay under the charge of having instigated the rebellion of the peasants, Wiklif put out his denial of transubstantiation. Lancaster, who suffered under a similar imputation, and who was formally cleared of the charge by a proclamation issued in the name of the king on July 3, 1381, forbad Wiklif from preaching this doctrine at Oxford. But the hierarchy were now thoroughly frightened. They again bade the University condemn him. That great and famous corporation peremptorily refused to do so.

In May, 1382, a council was held at Blackfriars, in preparation for which Wiklif put out a confession. The council, though seriously alarmed and disturbed by an earthquake, of which naturally enough, considering the temper of the times, Wiklif took advantage, condemned his errors. The archbishop now wrote to the chancellor, Dr. Rugge, commanding Wiklif's expulsion, in a letter dated May 30, 1382. The chancellor replied that no prelate whatsoever had any authority over the University, even in cases of heresy. Peter Stokes, the Carmelite friar, who came as the archbishop's commissary, was threatened with death if he did not cease to interfere.

On Corpus Christi day, June 5th, Philip Repyngdon went to the University church to preach before the chancellor, proctors, the mayor of Oxford, and other adherents of Wiklif. Here he uttered a furious invective against the Church and its rulers, stated that the authorities in the State were much better recommended in prayer than pope and bishop, and boasted that the Duke of Lancaster was the protector of the reformers. Peter Stokes, who forwarded the heads of the sermon to the archbishop on the next day, was afraid to leave the church, and adds that the chancellor and Repyngdon went laughing home. Repyngdon however was an unfaithful disciple, as other leaders have been unfaithful disciples, unstable partisans, for he recanted, was made Bishop of Lincoln in 1405, and in 1420 a cardinal. His successor in the see, Richard Fleming, had also been a Wiklifite. But he also recanted, and founded a college in Oxford for the express purpose of refuting Wiklif's doctrine. It is unsafe to create an institution for the purpose of maintaining particular tenets. This college was the foundation of which John Wesley was afterwards a fellow. It is possible that the college founded in honour of Keble may hereafter prepare students towards whose opinions the poet would have entertained the profoundest horror.

On June 9th, the archbishop bids Stokes return. He left on the 11th, and reached London the same evening. The 11th is the feast of St. Barnabas, and it is to be noted here, as it might be noted frequently elsewhere, that the medieval Church did not turn saints' days into days of rest. The chancellor and proctors instantly follow, are found to have favoured the Lollards, and are bidden to recant. The chancellor confesses his offence, and is pardoned at the intercession of William of Wykeham.

The archbishop bids the chancellor publish a decree, condemning Wiklif. The chancellor humbly answers that he dares not for his life. 'Why, you are a nest of heretics,' answers his Grace. However it is published, and the secular clergy clamour against the regulars, i. e. the monks, charging them with a wish to destroy the liberties of the University. In those days Carmelite friars were devoted adherents of Rome. But in those days also general councils were unpopular with popes, for they questioned even the pope's orthodoxy and morals, and had not yet progressed into canvassing the article of his infallibility. 'Many things,' said his friends to John

XXII, 'will be charged against you at the council' (of Constance). 'There is one worse fault than them all,' answered the pope; 'that I came over the Alps, and put myself before this council.' The poor chancellor, when the awe of the terrible archbishop's eye was not present, became again loyal to his supporters, and suspended one Crump, another friar, from his degree, for saying publicly that 'all Lollards are heretics.'

The king's uncles (for the king was only sixteen years old), in whose ears the shouts of that Smithfield mob are still ringing, before whose eyes Wat Tyler is still playing with the hilt of his dagger, and who are always talking in the royal writs of that 'detestable rebellion,' are at last compelled to interfere. On July 13, 1382, a missive is despatched to the chancellor and proctors, to the effect that Oxford is given over to heretical depravity, and that therefore an inquiry should be made by the regent graduates in theology and others. It speaks of certain conclusions which had been condemned by William (Courtenay) Archbishop of Canterbury, and it names John Wiklif, Nicolas Hereford, Philip Repyngdon, and John Aston as the most notable culprits. It forbids any one to harbour these persons on pain of expulsion, bids the authorities collect Wiklif's and Hereford's books as soon as possible, and to send them in a month's time, without correction or alteration, to the Archbishop of Canterbury. Disobedience to this writ is to be followed by the forfeiture of all liberties and privileges. The next day the king sends letters to the chancellor and proctors, bidding them restore Crump, whom they had suspended, and not to molest him should he attack Wiklif, Hereford, and Repyngdon.

It appears that the University bowed to this threat, displaced Rugge and the proctors, and proceeded to the election of a new chancellor. If I can identify Dr. William de Burton with the person of the same name who had been joint ambassador to Bruges eight years before, it is probable that the new chancellor was not particularly zealous in searching out the Wiklifites and their books. It is certain that the persecution was ineffectual in stopping the progress of these opinions. Six years passed, and another commission was issued for the purpose of checking the Lollards. In 1392 poor William Smith, the deformed preacher, whom slighted love had driven to become a devotee, a scribe, and a colporteur, was constrained to do penance, to deliver up his books, and to abandon an occupation which he had followed for eight years.

But a long time afterwards Archbishop Arundel declared that there were wild vines in the University, and therefore little grapes. On the other hand, there was published a testimony to Wiklif's merits, couched in the form of an academical decree, and sealed with the seal of the University. It was said that this decree was composed by Peter

Payne, Principal of St. Edmund Hall, and that the seal was affixed surreptitiously by the same personage. This real or fictitious decree was dated 1406. Four years later Arundel complains again that the University is always encouraging contumacy and rebellion, and sowing tares among the pure wheat; and again in the next year the same prelate declares, in a letter to the chancellor, that nearly the whole University is leavened with heretical pravity.

The tendencies of modern religious thought would rather induce men to say that Wiklif had lighted a torch which could never be put out. That his doctrines were sedulously embraced up to the time of the Reformation is charged against him by writers of the Roman, asserted to be his glory by those of the Reformed Church. The prelates attempted to crush him and his followers by acts of sanguinary ferocity; and Henry IV, who wanted allies, Henry V, who was a sincere enthusiast for the Church, and Henry VI, who was a devotee, were equally unfriendly to the Lollards, who seem, in part at least, to have discredited their religious character by turbulence, and even by conspiracy. Hence the disciples of Wiklif were proscribed in the statutes of King's College, Cambridge, founded by Henry VI.

Wiklif, it is said, retired to Lutterworth, where he died on the last day of the year 1384, as he was engaged in divine offices. The council of Constance anathematized him, and Bishop Fleming, who had been one of his followers, but was now zealous against him and his, dug up his bones, burnt them, and cast them into the brook which runs by Lutterworth. The enemies of his tenets commented on the manner of his death; his disciples laughed at the futile rage of the men who wreaked their vengeance on his remains, and said that 'cast into the brook they reached the sea, and that thus the whole world became his sepulchre, as all Christendom would be ultimately his convert.'

Besides his sermons and tracts, Wiklif, as is well known, translated the Latin Vulgate—then the only accessible text of the Scriptures—into the English language. He thus became the father of English prose, as Chaucer his contemporary was that of English verse, for in the year that Wiklif was made ambassador to Bruges, Chaucer got his annual gift of a cask of wine, and was appointed comptroller of the subsidies of wool, hides, and woolfells in London. Wiklif's theories of civil and church government have endured to our time, but the precedent which Courtenay established, of constraining the University to submit to ecclesiastical authority, did not fail of its fruit. Succeeding prelates and monarchs found out that there was no better way of checking free thought in the centres of intellectual activity than by subjecting the Universities to clerical control; and so Elizabeth sent her commissioners to expel Papists and Puritans; Laud applied himself, with his passionate bigotry and eager liking for detail, to the same task, and with considerable success.

Then, after the short-lived sway of the Puritans, the Act of Uniformity handed over by force of law these ancient institutions to ecclesiastical authority and intellectual darkness. To know what Oxford might be, we must search into the facts of those days, when, as Chancellor Rugge said, 'No prelate has any authority whatever in the University, even on matters of faith,' and must deliver Religion from the odious function of acting as the gaoler of intellectual energy.

WILLIAM LAUD.

WILLIAM LAUD.

The doom of a Church which resists or affronts the religious convictions of a people cannot be long delayed. That of a Church which allies itself with a caste, or a political party, or a social order, may be delayed indeed, but only for a time. Its existence will be prolonged as long as such a caste, party, or order finds that its establishment is useful, or that its maintenance is not damaging to its patrons or allies; as long indeed as no solid sacrifices are required in order to preserve it. When association with it is dangerous or inconvenient, they who have made it their tool, by affecting to be its champion, will suffer it to perish. A party is always ungrateful to its advocates when their work is done and their services are no longer necessary. But a political order is utterly indifferent to the most sacred institutions when they cease to be serviceable.

We need not appeal to recent history in support of these generalities. King and nobles made little stir against the downfal of the Church when the Long Parliament was resolved. On May 1, 1641, the Commons passed the Root and Branch Bill. On

June 8 the Lords rejected it, on the third reading. But on Feb. 5, 1642, after some remonstrances, the Lords passed a similar enactment, and the king assented. Nor did the Scotch nobility, in whose interest the episcopal establishment of the Restoration was created, make any energetic resistance to its disestablishment at the Revolution. And if the nobles of the United Kingdom have not been strenuous in defending ecclesiastical institutions, still less have they been willing to suffer for them. I am not aware that, since the Reformation, a single English nobleman has ever been a martyr, has ever shown any persistent devotion to the institutions in which he has been supposed to be peculiarly interested. But I know of a great many noblemen the foundation of whose fortunes was the wealth of the unreformed Church, of not a few who did not scruple to pillage the Church of the Reformation of much that monarch and parliament had left her. 'In the days of Mary,' says Michele the Venetian ambassador, 'the English in general'—he is speaking of the aristocracy and gentry whom he knew—'would turn Jews or Turks if their sovereign pleased; but the restoration of the abbey lands by the Crown keeps alive a constant fear among those who possess them.' In point of fact, establishments run two risks. They generally attach themselves to a party which is discredited by the people, and so provoke a larger hostility than their allies do; and they are invariably sacrificed to the fears, and it must be added to the cupidity, of those who have made tools of them. Furthermore. no reform, as far as I am aware, in religious establishments has been ever effected without bribing those who have pretended to be the patrons of such parts of the constitution. From the early days in which monasteries paid black mail to their bailiffs and advocates, down to the latest experience of compromise, clerical institutions have been alternately the defenders and the victims of a pliant and intelligent aristocracy. Of course, when there is a hurricane, and both are seriously imperilled, the chance of compromise is lost. But even in the French revolution, the wealth of the Church suffered more than the wealth of the nobles.

During the long reign of Elizabeth, according to the testimony of Bacon, the nation was generally inflamed with animosity towards Rome, and the clergy were generally with the nation. It is well known that the queen acted with great caution in dealing with the religious question after her accession, and was reputed to lag behind her people in resistance to Romish doctrine. It is true that she instantly restored the royal supremacy by act of parliament. She would have been untrue to the traditions and temper of her family had she not adopted this course, after the insolent manner in which Paul IV, to whom she had notified her accession, required her to submit her pretensions to his judgment and authority. But the queen's inclination seems to have tended towards the theological tenets of her father rather than to those of her brother; as indeed might have been expected from so imperious and resolute a character.

The clergy who ministered to the reformed religion were without suspicion of any Romish tendencies. The fires of Smithfield, and the flight to Germany, Holland and Switzerland, had markedly separated the advocates of the new system of Church government and faith from the adherents of the Roman see. The Protestant clergy were, moreover, incomparably more able and learned than their adversaries. Romanism prevailed in country districts only, and was kept alive there by the ministrations of some among the deprived clergy. Later on, the Catholics were stimulated to maintain their religion by emissaries, especially by those of the Society of Jesus. But most of the inhabitants of the towns were intensely Protestant. Among these Protestants, certain varieties of opinion, coeval with the accession of the queen, were ultimately developed into permanent differences.

Some of the exiles of Mary's reign had taken refuge with the German Protestants, others with the Swiss. The former were familiarised with the reforms of Luther, the latter with those of Calvin and his followers. Luther, partly perhaps from policy, since he had been countenanced by divers princes, partly it may be from real liking, partly it would seem from a wish to conciliate in matters which did not seem of intrinsic importance, retained much of the ceremonial of the older Church, and not a little of its mysticism. Calvin, on the other hand, who had taken refuge in a republican city, and who exercised in it the functions of a civil magistrate as much as those of an ecclesiastical reformer, had been far more thorough in his changes. He abandoned the ritual of the Roman Church, discarded its system of government, and utterly repudiated the mystical significance which it assigned to certain religious rites. But though his theory of a Church was framed on a republican model, he did not abate, in the person of those who administered such a Church, one jot of those ecclesiastical pretensions which the Roman see arrogated over its subjects. The authority of the presbyters in the Genevan school, of the Knoxes and Melvilles, who carried the tenets of that school to Scotland, was asserted as boldly and wielded as unsparingly as that of pope or legate.

As might have been expected, Elizabeth and her counsellors inclined, in resettling the English Reformation, to the tenets of Luther's theology. It was unlikely that a monarch, and especially a princess of the Tudor house, would acknowledge a republican form of Church government, particularly as it was certain, by its constitutional pretensions, to come into conflict with the civil power and the royal prerogative. Elizabeth had beyond doubt learned the lesson which Mary Stuart's reign and James the Sixth's minority taught so plainly.

Her heir-presumptive was a Catholic, and was, as long as she lived, the centre of reactionary intrigues. An act of Henry's Parliament had, it is true, settled the succession on the descendants of Mary Duchess of Suffolk. But the experience of Lady Jane Grey's brief reign proved that the hereditary title of Mary Stuart was certain to be respected. This title gave vitality to those machinations which formed, and still form, the sole apology for Mary's execution. To protect herself from foreign aggression and from the resistance of a proscribed sect at home, Elizabeth was forced, or thought she was forced, to persecute the Catholics; to maintain her prerogative, perhaps even to prevent civil government from being usurped by a convention of ambitious ecclesiastics, she was equally constrained to discourage, and finally to persecute, the Puritans. In those days no one dreamed of religious liberty. Perhaps, as Mr. Hallam has said, experience alone can fully demonstrate the safety of toleration. It was advocated, to be sure, by More in England, and by the Chancellor l'Hôpital in France. It generally has been recommended by the weaker parties in religious strife. But the stronger hardly acknowledge it even now.

Three centuries ago heresy, i. e. dissent from customary opinion on religious topics, was believed to be treason against the Divine Majesty, and to be punishable as treason, only in a more cruel and more symbolical way. To advocate toleration was to be called a Gallio. The quarrel of sects and opinions was a struggle for the mastery, in which no person was allowed to be neutral, and in which the vanquished were liable to the worst fortunes of war, to the fate of captives when no quarter is given. Had the advocates of the Genevan discipline gained the day, they would have proscribed the episcopal faction. Cartwright would have been as bitter in his discipline as Whitgift was; bitterer perhaps, because the appetite for persecution is marvellously sharpened in those who have been personally subjected to persecution. It is not a little singular, when our forefathers were searching after the precedents on which to found an apostolic Church, and were displaying no small amount of learning in stating the points of the controversy, that they did not discuss the case of Priscillian. This unfortunate personage, the first heretic who was delivered over to the secular power, was put to death by Maximus in 385 A.D., at the instance of two Spanish bishops, Idacius and Ithacius. The act was denounced by Martin of Tours and Ambrose, and the vindictive as well as ill-advised bishops were deposed. But the precedent was subsequently established and fully enlarged. It may be true, as the advocates of Elizabeth's policy aver, that those who denied the Supremacy suffered as traitors and not as heretics. To the victim, however, the choice between being burnt alive, as the latter, and being disembowelled alive, as the former, must have appeared, like all such alternatives, equally unpalatable. In modern times the credit of being the first to advocate the doctrine of toleration must be shared between the Independents and the Quakers. The last attempt to inflict civil penalties on those who think for themselves and their fellow men will probably be made by the inferior members of the Anglican hierarchy.

It cannot be doubted that queen and counsellors were wise, according to the obvious rules of human policy, in adopting the episcopal and discountenancing the presbyterian form of Church government. Associated with hereditary nobles as peers of parliament, the bishops of Elizabeth's day had also great judicial power, for they held courts in which they dispensed penalties without the presence of assessors and without the intervention of a jury. Together they formed the Upper House of Convocation, an institution which the Tudor princes employed to give a legal sanction to their acts of spiritual despotism, at least over the clergy. A committee of their order formed a still more formidable tribunal, under the name of a High Commission Court; and some of them were associated with another engine of prerogative, the Star Chamber. They might have been, as Bacon allows, the successors of the Apostles, 'but in some particulars,' he adds, 'they were more like the successors of Diotrephes, who loved to have the preeminence.'

But they were none the less obsequious servants

of the queen. If they ferreted out priests and recusants, and harried preachers and Puritans, they were submissive to her Grace. To do them justice, they were fully informed of the importance of submission. She never spared threats when they seemed to have a will of their own. She told Cox that she would unfrock him when he demurred to some extortion which one of her courtiers wished to practise on him. She suspended Grindal from his functions when he hesitated to use sharp measures with the Puritans. She encouraged her dependants in depriving the Church of its lands. As Hatton pillaged the see of Ely in order to build his town house, so Cecil enlarged the demesne of Burleigh by despoiling the Bishop of Peterborough. She told the bishops in 1584 that if they did not amend matters she would depose them. She suspended one Bishop of London for marrying a widow, and resented the sermon of another who had inveighed against female vanity, for she threatened that she would fit the preacher for heaven by taking away his staff and mantle.

Now such ecclesiastics were convenient servants as well as energetic agents. The monarch was actually, as one of them declared metaphorically, the breath of their nostrils. There was no fear of resistance from men whose revenues and whose risk of losing them were perpetual pledges of fidelity. I am not aware that the episcopal order has ever shown much interest in the fortunes or much consideration for the opinions of the inferior clergy. But the bishops of the Elizabethan era were least of all given to this generosity. They ruled their subjects, to be sure, with a rough hand. Parker chastised them with whips; Whitgift with scorpions; while Bancroft emulated the vigour of his predecessor.

On the other hand, it must be allowed that the Puritans of Elizabeth's time were as stubborn and unyielding as their masters were. They ruled in the Universities, under Humphreys at Oxford, Cartwright at Cambridge. Elizabeth sometimes displaced the most intractable by the hands of her commissioners. But in these Universities the direct influence of the bishop has always been small. The academics have always by charter and by custom looked with suspicion on episcopal interference, or have actively resisted it. In the towns, too, the most eminent and influential ministers were on the same side. The country gentlemen, especially after the Roman Catholics were excluded from parliament, were more and more inclined to Puritan sentiments, and in spite of Elizabeth's threats and rebukes, more and more persistently demanded those reforms in Church and State which would bring the ecclesiastical administration more closely in accordance with the Genevan model. The ministers preached, the congregations practised what they heard: both suffered, and both proved how impolitic Elizabeth's administration of Church affairs was, by their increasing strength and increasing boldness. They called the Press to their aid, and strove to accumulate detestation on the bishops, whom they hated and despised, by the coarse and virulent attacks of Martin Marprelate. The defence of the episcopal order and the apology for the polity of the Anglican Church was supplied by Hooker, who attempted, and with no little success, to sustain the cause which he advocated on grounds of reason, and to seek for the foundation of the ecclesiastical system in the permanent laws of civil government. This great writer, who is nowhere a partisan, and, almost alone among theological authors, invariably treats the topic which he handles with fairness and candour, gave and still gives the ablest defence of the Anglican Church as a part of the social constitution of the kingdom. He was able to argue with sufficient cogency, both from the inevitable tendency of Puritan opinion, and from the positive statements of Puritan partisans, that the necessary consequence of accepting Puritan principles would be the subjection of the civil power to ecclesiastical authority. For it should be remembered, that in those days no system of Church government comprehended the toleration of any other, none failed to claim for itself the aid of the civil magistrate in enforcing its own decrees and extirpating its rivals. The choice was either the administration of Whitgift and his suffragans, or the rule of Cartwright and the Presbyteries.

The statesmen of Elizabeth's day, though they

would probably have maintained the episcopal system as the safest and most politic form of Church government, were not disinclined to give as much support as possible to the Puritan party. Leicester, vain, greedy, and treacherous as he was, was their avowed patron. So were Walsingham, Cecil, Knollys, the wisest and most trustworthy of Elizabeth's counsellors. There were many motives which might have led them to such a policy. There is a standing quarrel between the civil and the ecclesiastical administration, which appears perpetually in the history of modern Europe. The queen cared only to maintain her prerogative in Church and State. Her lay counsellors were, on the other hand, interested in preventing the hierarchy from subjecting the laity under pretence of checking heresy and schism. And we may conclude that the more shrewd and far-seeing of Elizabeth's advisers were unwilling to drive into disaffection those who were among the most loyal subjects of the queen, because they entertained honest scruples on subjects which, at that time, reformed Churches conceived to be unessential differences of conduct or discipline. It was plain that there were other and more vital points at issue between the Reformation and the see of Rome, and that the forces of the former should be counselled to unity and concession. The last crusade which the pope has preached, the Thirty Years' War, was imminent, though lingering; and every wise man must have foreseen that the effort after recovering the universal empire of Christendom would not be made by the Jesuits only, but would take the form of a struggle between the gigantic power of Spain, Austria, and of the pope on the one hand, and of Protestant Europe on the other. And in the end, the conclusion of the contest was exhaustion.

The English people, towards the conclusion of Elizabeth's reign, hated the pope with an almost universal fervour. During the stormy days of the last Edward the administration was in the hands of a gang of adventurers, and the vessel of State was without rudder, compass, or steersman. It is easy to account for the reaction which gave Mary her hereditary right, and which was patient under the discipline of her ferocious piety, even though she summoned five parliaments in as many years. Elizabeth, more wisely, summoned only one, and that in the first year of her reign, for nearly the same length of time.

Persecuted, but not dismayed, the English Puritans looked forward to the succession of James with patient hope. He had been carefully brought up in the Protestant faith, and was familiar with the discipline of Geneva. Hence, on his progress from Scotland, the dissatisfied ministers presented him with the famous Millenary petition, the name implying that the instrument was signed by a thousand persons. In reality the signatures were eight hundred and twenty-five in number. The petition prayed for certain relaxations in points not yet deemed vital, and for a revival of discipline. Although James had made no secret of his real feelings on the question of Church government, he so far acceded to the prayer of the petitioners as to consent to the Hampton Court Conference. Perhaps he anticipated that such an assemblage would be a convenient arena in which to exhibit his polemical powers, which were indeed by no means contemptible, though far inferior to what his conceit valued them at.

But in point of fact, James had no liking for presbyteries. He had been scolded and rated by them from his youth up, and long familiarity had not made the discipline more pleasant. As Elizabeth had watched his troubles and profited by his experience, so he had seen her success, and longed for a more courteous clergy. It was not that he entertained any good feeling towards Rome, but he was able to comprehend the *via media* of the English establishment, which had been schooled into a profound deference to the prerogative by its vigorous and astute mistress. Besides, he recognised its consummate usefulness to a ruler who believed that he had divine rights as a monarch, and a transcendent knowledge of the mystery of kingcraft. Nor did his bishops disabuse him of this conviction. They speedily took to calling him the English Solomon, as State bishops are wont to extol the wisdom and expound the virtue of princes. They administered to him the most copious doses of flattery, doses which he swallowed naturally, and as of right. Whitgift fell on his knees before him at the Hampton Court Conference, and declared, amidst a band of approving suffragans, 'that the prince spoke by the Spirit of God.' The witness who relates this piece of profanity adds, 'I wist not what they meant, but the spirit was rather foul-mouthed.' Now Whitgift's language was very different from the rough, uncourtly rebukes of the Scottish preachers; and we need not wonder that, with such a complaisant hierarchy, James felt he had reason for his adage, 'No bishop, no king.'

But while his courtiers and his prelates flattered him, the nation, and especially the disappointed Puritans, passed from dissatisfaction to disgust, and at last to contempt. Court divines spoke of his predecessor as a bright occidental star, and of him as the sun in his strength, and stuck this nauseous nonsense into the preface of the new Bible. But those who did not live in, or by his favours, were at a loss to distinguish the majesty of Solomon in a middle-aged, red-faced, sandy-haired man, whose chin was scantily bearded, who slobbered while he gabbled his uncouth mother-tongue, and whose legs were hardly able to support him. The English chivalry had no respect for a king who not only had no courage, but who affected cowardice, and whose very wife despised him. The decorous courtiers of Elizabeth were disgusted at his coarse affection towards his young Scotch favourite, the infamous Carr; at his gross familiarities; and at the filthiness of his talk. The Puritans were irritated beyond measure at the affront which he put upon them by publishing the Book of Sports, though it was not till the reign of his successor that the crowning insult of compelling its use was committed. He vexed the trader and the public with monopolies; the whole nation by his foreign policy and alliances; for his infatuated pride led him to dally with the Spanish marriage, and, as was believed, to enter into an understanding with the pope. Apologists in later times, who estimate facts from a modern point of view, have laboured to rehabilitate the reputation of James. His contemporaries believed him to be a vainglorious and awkward pedant, a false, coarse, cowardly despot. We are told by one who witnessed his progress from Holyrood to Theobald's, that he had not finished it before the admiration of the intelligent world was turned to contempt. During the twenty-two years of his reign he did his best to extinguish admiration and to exaggerate contempt.

I have already observed that the Universities were the stronghold of Puritanism, and that they especially favoured the creed of Augustin as interpreted by Calvin. He was a bold man who dared, during Elizabeth's reign, to utter from the pulpit of either church of St. Mary any doubts as to predestination and election, or showed any tendency towards the milder tenets of Arminius. It was only a slender party which was beginning to look with contempt on foreign reformed Churches, and was insisting on the necessity of episcopal government and episcopal ordination as a fundamental condition of Christianity. But among the earliest of these separatists was William Laud.

This man, whom many have considered a martyr and saint, and as many a meddling and mischievous fool, who deserved the fate which he provoked, was born at Reading on Oct. 7, 1573. He was the only son of William Laud, a clothier, his mother having been the widow of another clothier, John Robinson. No industry in those days was more honourable and none more general than that of a clothier, or, as we should now say, a woollen manufacturer; none which had been more encouraged by kings and parliaments. Laud the father, we are informed, kept many spinners, weavers, and fullers in his employment. Being no doubt a man of substance, he sent his son as a commoner to St. John's College, Oxford, which had been lately founded by Sir Thomas White, a merchant taylor, and put under the protection of the Company of Merchant Taylors. White allotted two of the places in his College to Reading. In pursuance of this ordinance, the Mayor and Corporation nominated young Laud to one of their places in 1590, after he had been a year at Oxford. He soon made himself known in his University; 'for though,' says Antony Wood, ' he was little of stature, he was a very froward, confident, and zealous person.' In the last year of the seventeenth century he took orders; in 1603 he was Proctor. After filling several livings in succession, he was elected (though not without a severe contest, and an appeal to the king) President of his College in 1611. In the same year, George Abbot, who had watched Laud's career in Oxford and elsewhere with great suspicion, was made Archbishop of Canterbury, by the influence of Chancellor Ellesmere and the Earl of Dunbar. Unhappily for himself, Laud was immediate successor in the primacy.

Among the relics of its unlucky President which are kept by St. John's College, Oxford, and with religious care, is a diary, written by Laud himself. It begins with the date of his birth, and is continued to within a year or more of his death. The entries of the first part (for the notes now bound into one small volume are plainly divisible into two portions) were probably made during the space of about thirty years, that is, from his election to the headship of his College till his imprisonment. The diary was published in 1694, in order to illustrate Laud's character. It was certainly not intended for any eye besides the writer's own. But some extracts from the book had been previously printed; and it is from these, culled carefully by an unfriendly hand, that Macaulay justifies the contempt with which he treats Laud. After the archbishop was committed to prison, the volume was placed in the hands of Prynne, who prefixed certain selections from its contents to an elaborate and huge work which he compiled on the conduct of Laud in Church and State, under the odd title of a Breviate of his life.

Prynne was a barrister of vast learning and intense Puritanism. He had graduated at Oriel College, Oxford. He was as diligent as he was learned. The titles of his numerous works are alone sufficient for a pamphlet. It may be added, that he was dull beyond parallel. He had no more critical power than the compiler of a peerage has. He wrote on Parliaments, on the administration of Laud, in defence of the Monarchy as an institution, against the Hierarchy, and against Stage-players. The last named was one of his earliest works, and brought him into serious trouble. He was supposed, in a passage which described women players in a phrase of round coarseness, to have glanced at the queen, who, it appears, took part in a mask, some weeks after the Histriomastix was published. He was sentenced, after the fashion of the day, to lose his ears and to be imprisoned. When in prison he wrote a libel on Laud, which the bishop forwarded to Noy, the notorious attorney-general of Ship-money reputation. Noy had Prynne brought before him, and asked him whether he had written the letter. 'How can I tell,' said Prynne, 'unless I see it.' Noy put the letter into his hands, and he immediately tore it up, and threw the fragments out of the window. For this he was again brought before the Star Chamber, where Laud, according to the diary, interceded for him.

Four years after this occurrence, Prynne, in company with Bastwick a physician and Burton a clergyman, was brought before the Star Chamber on a charge of libelling the hierarchy. The culprits were sentenced to the customary punishment. One of the Lords, turning up Prynne's hair and viewing the fragments which had been left by the discipline of 1634, expressed his indignation that a second amputation was possible. It would have been more natural for him to have congratulated the Star Chamber on the fact that their favourite penalty could be reiterated on so incorrigible a Puritan, and to have expressed a hope that the hangman might yet leave sufficient cartilage for a future occasion. The culprits were sent to distant prisons. One of the first acts of the Long Parliament was to release these men, and to select one of them as their agent in stating the case of the Commons against Laud.

The diary is ludicrous enough in many particulars, and Prynne, though no humourist, had the wit to select those entries which were most damaging to Laud's reputation. Among these are some of the many dreams which Laud records. Thus, he sees a vision of the Lord Keeper (Williams), to whom Laud owed his first advancement, but with whom he now had a quarrel. The dreamer thought that his rival was dead, and that he passed by while some men were erecting a monument for him, and that they said that the dead man's lower lip was 'infinitely swollen and fallen.' The same day he met the Duke of Buckingham, and found some part of his vision realised, for he writes that 'the Lord Keeper had strangely forgotten himself to the duke, and was dead in his affections already.' Again, he dreams that he saw the Lord Keeper in chains, a vision which Laud contrived to fulfil afterwards. The king appears, too, in these manifestations. 'I dreamed,' he says, under date of Oct. 14, 1636, 'marvellously that the king was offended with me, and would cast me off, and give me no cause.' And again, under Feb. 12, 1639, the ivory gate is again opened, to tell him that King Charles is to be married to a minister's widow. 'I,' writes Laud, 'was called to do it; but no service-book could be found, and lo, in my own there was no office for the order of marriage.' Mixed with this rubbish are some scraps of astrology, in which, it must be admitted, half the educated, and all the uneducated, classes believed, and certain notes about the seasons and the weather.

How Prynne must have chuckled when he read, under August 4, 1633, the following entry, after a statement that his Grace of Canterbury (Abbot) died on this day, and that the king offered Laud the see: 'On that very morning at Greenwich there came one to me, presently, and that avowed ability to perform it, and offered me to be a cardinal. I went presently to the king, and acquainted him both with the thing and with the person.' And again, on the 17th of the same month: 'I had a serious offer made me again to be a cardinal. I was then from Court, but as soon as I came thither, which was Wednesday, Aug. 21, I acquainted his Majesty with it. But my answer again was, that somewhat dwelt within me which would not suffer that, till Rome were other than it is.' Now, in our own time such an offer made to an English prelate would be looked on as excessively suspicious, nor would the recorded manner of Laud's refusal have aided in removing the suspicion. But in the days of the Long Parliament it was clear proof that Laud meditated the subjugation of the English conscience to popery, as he counselled the violation of the liberties and fortunes of England by the prerogative; that the High Commission Court would be the prelude of the Inquisition, the Star Chamber of the Spanish tyranny. The memory of the policy of Alva and the fate of the Netherlands was still fresh in the minds of Englishmen; and at the time of the Long Parliament, after eleven years forced cessation from public business, after Eliot had been slowly murdered in the Tower, and the people had suffered arbitrary taxation, and honest men had been tortured and imprisoned, and soldiers had been billetted on private houses, and a thousand horrors had been practised, the whole community was in a ferment, and exaggerated the forces arrayed against its liberties.

There are two sides to Laud's public character, which, to do him justice, must be distinguished. Had he never mixed himself up with politics, had he even played a subordinate part in the political history of his time, he would have had as respectable a reputation as any man of the seventeenth century. There was nothing sordid in his nature. He was above any charge of corruption. If he was a fool, he was honest. His industry was constantly mischievous, his abilities were contemptible, but he was diligent and well-meaning. Nor can any man charge him with perfidy. From the hour that he was taken into the counsels of James, to that of his death on Tower-hill, he never broke faith or swerved from the few principles which he comprehended. He was neither knave nor coward. His character — apart from his political career — is praised by May; his courage and constancy at his trial by Prynne. He never abated one jot of his pretensions when he stood before his judges, and fearlessly asserted his good faith to Church and King, while he avowed the principles on which he had acted. Those principles, it is true, have been repudiated by every man of sense in our day. In Laud's time, men far abler than himself advocated them and acted on them. But Laud's highest praise lies in his patronage of Letters.

Among the contents of the diary to which I have already referred is a page on both sides of which Laud has written down the public objects which he had before him, and which he strove to fulfill. He was a munificent benefactor to his College, and to the charities of his native town, for he enriched

St. John's, and founded an almshouse in Reading. He induced Charles to bestow such Irish tithes as were impropriated to the Treasury on the Irish Church. He repaired St. Paul's, and settled an estate on the cathedral, in order that it might be kept in constant repair. He strove to augment the income of the poorer sees, which had been grievously dilapidated by corrupt bishops and rapacious courtiers in Elizabeth's time, and sought to effect a settlement of the London tithes between the clergy and the city.

But his most enduring benefits were conferred on the University of Oxford. Here he was the munificent patron of learning, and especially of Oriental studies. At vast pains and expense he collected for Bodley's library 1300 manuscripts of the rarest and most precious character. He founded a Professorship of Arabic at Oxford, poorly indeed, for the troubles came when the endowment was inchoate. In order to disseminate learning, he established a Greek press in London, and contemplated the maintenance of another in Oxford. And all this work was done at his own charges.

Nor did he confine his favours to his creatures and the partisans of his policy. Laud was ambitious, and in his clumsy way intriguing, but he was not vindictive, nor was he incapable of discerning merit in any but those who followed or flattered him. He could forgive his opponents, if they could prove their acquaintance with the learning which he strove to foster. He pensioned Chillingworth, and gave a canonry at Windsor to Hales, though his tenets were wholly averse to those which the former entertained, while the latter actually crossed him. It speaks little for the Long Parliament, that it persecuted both these worthies. But it is not difficult to find examples of intolerant bigotry in our own time, of malignity to which Laud was wholly superior, in persons who cannot allege Laud's excuse. With vastly inferior means for beneficence, Laud strove to emulate the munificence of the medieval prelates, the Wykehams, Waynefletes, Chicheles, Foxes, and Wolseys.

It is impossible, however, to judge Laud by these incidents alone, honourable as this part of his public career was. In his time religion and politics had been made one, and he chose his side. It was not convenient indeed at that time to have chosen any other side than that of the Court. But Laud did his best to embitter the nation with the Church and the monarchy. He succeeded, in concert with others, to an extent which has not been paralleled since. He engendered a hatred to the hierarchy which must have gone far beyond his expectations. It may be true, as an eminent partisan has implied, that a good Churchman is always the advocate of privilege, always the foe of public liberty. But such excellence in a Churchman is a serious detriment to a Church.

In the early part of his career, Laud committed a grave blunder. A younger brother of Lord

Mountjoy fell in love with Lady Penelope Devereux, a daughter of the unlucky Earl of Essex, and the parties pledged themselves privately to each other. But the lady's relatives would not hear of an alliance with a younger son, and therefore constrained her to marry Lord Rich. In time the younger son succeeded to his brother's peerage and estate. Before or after this, the lady contrived to inform her old lover that her affection towards him was unimpaired. In consequence, events occurred which enabled Lord Rich to procure a divorce in the ecclesiastical courts. This process, however, did not allow either party to marry again. But Laud married the lady and her old lover, and apologised, when censured, by saying that he thought the private contract was binding, and that therefore the previous marriage was void. For some time this irregular act was an obstacle to Laud's advancement.

In 1616 he was made Dean of Gloucester, and in the next year he accompanied James to Scotland. Here Laud commenced that policy which ultimately became his ruin. He repaired the chapel at Holyrood, and adopted a splendid ritual in it. The Scotch bishops, whose precarious influence over their presbyteries was imperilled by this proceeding of the English chaplain, were alarmed and remonstrated. James, with his customary wisdom, told them that he was bringing some English theologians to enlighten their minds. With equal consideration, he haughtily declined to argue with other remonstrants, and met their objections by fine and imprisonment; a course of procedure which the foolish bigot who has written the latest Life of Laud, one Lawson, describes as politic. It was not wonderful therefore that the people refused to accept the five articles which James wished to thrust on them; and, on the other hand, it was natural that Laud, whose obstinacy was stimulated by opposition, urged the king to impose a liturgy on the Scottish Church. Twenty years later, the temporary success of this project gave force to the convulsion which overthrew the English Church, liturgy, primate and all.

On Laud's return to England he contrived to gain the countenance of Buckingham. Through the joint influence of the favourite and Williams, bishop-designate of Lincoln and Lord Keeper, Laud was in 1621 advanced to the bishopric of St. David's, and from this time was constantly at Court, and employed as a minister. He was made chaplain to Buckingham, and took credit to himself that though the favourite's mother, after the well-known spiritual tournament with Fisher the Jesuit, abandoned the English for the Roman Church, her son remained stanch to the reformed creed. But Buckingham's religion must have been of the flimsiest material, if we are to admit that there is a necessary connexion between faith and works.

At this time George Abbot was Archbishop of Canterbury. This prelate, who occupied the see for twenty-two years, was a leader and patron of the

Puritan party. As head of an Oxford College and Vice-Chancellor of the University he had always looked on Laud with little favour, and was supposed to have hindered his preferment.

In the spring of 1621 Abbot went on a visit to Lord Zouch, and took the diversion of shooting with a cross-bow at the deer in Bramshall Park. One of Lord Zouch's keepers, though he had been repeatedly warned to be cautious, got within the range of the primate's bolt and was shot dead on the spot. Abbot was filled with the greatest grief at this unlucky accident. But his enemies or rivals instantly took advantage of it. Williams urged that the primate had forfeited his estate to the Crown by this casual homicide, and that he must by the canon law be suspended from all his ecclesiastical functions. He had reason afterwards to regret that he ever recommended the suspension of a brother bishop. The king, to do him justice, instantly wrote to the archbishop, said that an angel might have miscarried in that sort, and declared that he would not touch a penny of his estate. It was thought expedient, however, that a commission should issue to inquire into the circumstances. The commissioners cleared Abbot; but to obviate any possible objection, the king issued a formal pardon to the primate. Abbot ever afterwards, with true Christian humility, kept the day as a solemn fast. He immediately settled an annuity of £20 on the widow, 'a sum,' says Fuller, 'which soon got her another husband.'

This accident, however, diminished the influence and lowered the reputation of the primate. Laud and Williams immediately took advantage of the odium which they wished to strengthen, by refusing to receive consecration at his hands. They induced Spelman, who united the learning of a profound antiquary to the superstition of a narrow bigot—no rare combination—to write a book on the subject, in which he argued that Abbot had forfeited his spiritual functions by the occurrence. They hoped to compel his resignation, if not his degradation; since Abbot was not only averse to the tenets of the new school of theology, but as he showed afterwards, in his refusal to license a sermon of one Sibthorp, had no sympathy with the slavish doctrine which the clergy preached. For Sibthorp had held that the Parliament had no right to refuse the king money, and that its discretion lay solely in the discovery of the easiest and most equitable means by which the tax should be distributed.

Abbot, as he tells us, in order to obviate the influence of Somerset, introduced George Villiers to the king. The rapidity with which this man rose to the post of chief favourite to James, and the confidence which Charles reposed in him, are matters of familiar history. He raised and ruined men at his pleasure. He elevated Bacon, and suffered him to fall. He quarrelled with Middlesex, the Lord Treasurer, and furthered his impeachment by the Commons. He was bishop-maker in general; for as long as his power endured, he filled the sees with his creatures and flatterers, as noble bishop-makers generally do. His influence was exerted to bring about the Spanish match. His caprice or offended vanity broke it off, and drove the nation into a war with Spain, which was as unnecessary as were the overtures to amity with her. The Commons, who had re-established their right of impeachment in the cases of Bacon and Middlesex, would have assuredly hunted him down in the end, had not Felton's dagger superseded their prosecution.

It is known that James was weary of his favourite, and would have gladly rid himself of Buckingham in the later years of his life, had he been able to undergo the effort. He even entered into a correspondence with Somerset, after giving that infamous person a full pardon, and listened to the grave charges which he made against his rival and successor. It is possible that Williams may have learned something about this correspondence, and have therefore acted with less than customary deference to Buckingham. It is certain that he was out of the favourite's goodwill before the end of the year 1622, if we can trust, as it is clear we may in this case, Laud's diary. But either because Williams was really useful, or because the king was too indolent to make any change in his ministers, the Lord Keeper retained his place for a few months after the death of James. He was then rudely dismissed, and Coventry was put in his office. Williams never regained any influence till it was too late.

'A cashiered courtier,' says Hacket, speaking of his friend and patron, 'is like an almanack of the last year, remembered by nothing but the great eclipse.'

Williams would have been an incomparably wiser counsellor than Laud. He would never have advised those violent and repressive measures which only pent up the forces under which king, aristocracy, Church and Liturgy were overwhelmed at last. He was, (if we can anticipate a word which became familiar a generation later, and then in a far more pronounced sense than could be understood at the beginning of Charles's reign,) a Whig in politics. He would have used the customary machinery of government for the purpose of compromise and conciliation; would have thrown in his lot with the Hydes, the Falklands, and the Seldens, rather than with the reactionary bishops and the Court. That he was dissatisfied with Laud's measures is unquestionable, for he refused to persecute the Puritans in his diocese; that Laud knew him to be dissatisfied, is proved from the scandalous prosecution to which he subjected his rival in the Star Chamber. The mere fact that Osbaldistone had sent certain letters to Williams, in which he had given the primate a few contemptuous nicknames, such as 'little urchin,' 'meddling hocus pocus,' and so forth, could never have justified the procedure by which a man, who had held high office, who was at least for capacity and character one of the most respectable among the statesmen of the age, as well as being by his profession attached to the king's party, was fined £5000 to the king, £3000 to the archbishop, and imprisoned during pleasure. Williams lay in the Tower for three years, and was released only at the beginning of the Long Parliament, when Laud took his place in prison.

This prosecution of Williams is one of the worst of Laud's acts, for it is one of signal ingratitude, since he owed his first elevation to the former Lord Keeper. Williams of course resented the wrong, and detested the doer of it. What he thought of his rival is to be seen in the manuscript notes appended by him to Laud's speech on the punishment of Bastwick, Burton, and Prynne, notes which are quite as savage, but not so witty, as those of Swift on Burnet. But it is a habit with ambitious ecclesiastics to slander, malign, undermine their brethren, especially when they think they can prove their own orthodoxy by the process, or vindicate their fidelity to existing institutions. Late experience has taught us that this treacherous bitterness may exist in the calmer breasts of lawyers, and even constitute the motive of their lives.

The death of Buckingham, the seclusion of Abbot, and the disgrace of Williams left Laud in the undisputed possession of the post which he had laboured for, that of Charles's first minister and confidant. So rapid a rise from the deanery of Gloucester, 'that shell without a kernel,' as James described it (according to the diary,) to the post of chief favourite, was sure to provoke emulation, as well as envy. Clergymen who discerned that the road to the king's favour through his minister was to profess unbounded devotion to the prerogative, and the Book of Sports, and sacerdotalism, and the new creed of London House, were not slow to improve the opportunity. Montague, bishop of Chichester, dallied with the Roman see in the Church, and 'appealed to Cæsar' in the State. Goodman of Gloucester died in the Roman communion. Laud avowed that, in dispensing patronage, he should prefer celibate to married priests. Sibthorp and Manwaring, as Wentworth said, before he was corrupted by Straffordism, 'preached in their pulpits as gospel that the king can take his subjects' money, and damned those who refuse it.'

It is well known that the House of Commons took umbrage at these clerical politicians, and that in particular they attacked Montague and Manwaring. But their action against these clergymen was emphatically overruled by the king. Under Charles, to be censured by Parliament was the surest road to preferment. The House condemned Manwaring to be disabled from holding any ecclesiastical dignity, and the king instantly gave him the deanery of Worcester, and subsequently the bishopric of St. David's. Montague was made bishop of Chichester, though not without remonstrance, for one Jones, a bookseller, exhibited charges against him at St. Mary-le-Bow. The protest was rejected, because 'it was not preferred in the manner prescribed by law.' Some years afterwards, when the bishops were at a discount, Jones was invited to restate his charges, to Montague's disadvantage.

No part of English history is better known than that of the first four years of the reign of Charles. Between May 17, 1625, and March 10, 1629, Charles summoned and met three Parliaments. The first declined to grant a supply before the nation's grievances were considered, and was dissolved on August 12. The second, summoned for Feb. 6, 1626, sat till June 15, when, despite the remonstrance of the Lords, the Parliament was dissolved anew; for the Commons insisted on maintaining their privileges, before they would relieve the king's necessities. After a council held on Jan. 29, 1627, in which Sir Robert Cotton advised the calling of another Parliament, a third is summoned for March 17, 1628. It carries the Petition of Right, and grants a supply. It is prorogued on June 26, meeting again on Jan. 20, 1629. It treats of Tonnage and Poundage, of Jesuits and Arminians, of the king's interference with its debates, of his private instructions to Finch the Speaker. Then comes the scene between Eliot and Holles, Selden and Strode on the one hand, and the Speaker on the other. This happened on the 2nd of March, and on the 10th the third Parliament was dissolved.

The Commons had reason for their suspicions, for at the beginning of the second session, Sir Thomas Wentworth, who had been a leader on the popular side, had suddenly deserted it for the king's party, through the agency of Weston, Earl of Portland, the Treasurer. He had been imprisoned for refusing to pay an illegal tax in 1627. He had been a confessor of the Constitution; he was now about to turn traitor to it. Such apostacies were not rare, but none was more notable. Pym knew what his abilities were, and divined how he would use them. He was well aware that an apostate always tries to atone for his previous creed by thoroughgoing hostility to it. Wentworth had been their confidant, he was now to be their enemy, with the advantage of knowing their policy and their tactics. The profession of Christianity, it is said, embraces three sects — Protestants, Catholics, and Converts. A similar division may be made of political opinion and partisanship. And so, in that spirit of prophecy which comes from profound sagacity and clearness of vision, Pym said to the great renegade, 'You are going to be undone, but remember, that though you leave us now, I will never leave you while your head is on your shoulders.' For twelve years he brooded over the threat, and at last fulfilled it to the letter.

The king, reinforced by so energetic a counsellor, hastened to take vengeance. Several members of the late Parliament were seized, among them Eliot, Selden, and Holles. The first of these patriots, a man of singular gentleness, piety, and courage, was deemed the chief offender. The story of his long imprisonment, of his pining sickness, of his love to the home from which he was torn, of his pathetic death, of his religious fortitude, is told in detail, and with touching fidelity, by Mr. Forster. England has her political martyrs, yet none of them occupies a higher place than this pure-hearted and generous champion of public liberty. But when Charles had wasted away that noble life he had not sated his vengeance, for he refused the small boon that Eliot's bones should be laid in the place which he loved. 'Let Sir John Eliot,' he wrote at the foot of the petition which was presented to him by his victim's family, 'be buried in the church of the parish where he died.' The dignity of the king's own death, the reaction which restored a family and resuscitated a hierarchy, and perhaps the contrast between the characters of the first and second Charles, have canonized the friend of Buckingham, the Royal Martyr. But there were days in which Charles Stuart was believed to be a perfidious, cruel, and vindictive tyrant. Even Cottington could write to Wentworth, 'Your old dear friend Eliot is like to die.' He made no comment on his murderer.

No reputation stood higher than that of Selden. He was respected on all sides as an honest man, and as a constitutional lawyer to whom there was no rival. He had little mind to be a martyr, but he had still less a mind to be a knave. It was certain that an act must have been wholly indefensible when he was ready to energetically condemn it. He was equally beloved by Laud and Williams. It is almost impossible to believe that the attack on him was dictated by anything but the king's ungovernable temper and bitter vindictiveness. Nor was the character of those other gentlemen inferior on whom Charles poured his wrath. A tardy restitution was made them, in a form which legal pedantry allowed to be constitutional; for on November 23, 1667, the House of Commons resolved 'that the judgment, 5 Charles I, against Sir John Eliot, Denzil Holles, and B. Valentine, in the King's Bench, was an illegal judgment, and against the freedom and privilege of Parliament.' The Lords, on the motion of Holles, now a peer, affirmed the same resolution on December 11.

The king resolved to have no more Parliaments. In order to render domestic despotism possible and continuous, it was necessary to have no wars. In order to carry on the government, it was necessary to find money. Money could not be obtained lawfully, but it possibly might be got under colour of law. The receipts of the Exchequer from the Star Chamber fines were casual, and though prodigiously oppressive to the victims, gave but a small revenue in the aggregate. The inquisition of the royal forests afforded some funds; but the enormous confiscations which the Treasury levied on peers and gentlemen of estate were small sources of royal income. Yet they gave rise to great dissatisfaction. Thus the Earl of Salisbury was fined £20,000 for encroaching.

Thereafter, an Earl of Salisbury was in his place in the House of Lords early in the year 1645, and early in 1649. Then the king constrained people to take knighthood, or pay a fine. He revived also the custom of granting monopolies, though such grants were made illegal by a statute of James the First. But the great invention of the hour was Noy's expedient of ship-money.

Noy, like Strafford, was an apostate. In the early part of the reign he had been associated with Selden as counsel for those who had refused to pay the illegal loan which was levied by the Council, and recommended by the clergy from their pulpits. Now, however, he had deserted to the Crown, and was attorney-general. He was, like many men of the time, a profound but not very critical antiquary. Examining the records in the Tower, he found that certain sea-ports, and even maritime counties, had been occasionally called on to contribute ships for the public service in the days of the early Plantagenets. In searching records I have myself recognized payments made to the Crown for the same and similar purposes, and these even from inland counties. But the impost was none the less illegal. It was contrary to the tenor of the Great Charter. It violated a thousand enactments and precedents by which the Great Charter was sustained. Even if it did apply to certain towns and counties, assuredly it did not cover all these divisions. Even if the whole realm were liable to the tax on an emergency, it could not be claimed as a substitute for all taxes, for the ordinary purposes of the sovereign's revenue, and for totally different ends from those of protecting the seas with an armed marine. It is possible, as Mr. Hallam has argued, that, as Noy died soon after his reputed discovery, he did not contemplate the use which would be made of his information. But he must have known that the precedent was not law, and could not be justified on any constitutional ground whatsoever. Noy died on August 10, 1634, and the first writs for ship-money were issued in October of the same year.

These writs alluded to depredations committed by pirates, stated that it was necessary during a time of general war that money should be provided, and bade London and the other sea-ports assess themselves for the supply of a certain number of ships of a prescribed tonnage and a proper equipment. London remonstrated, but in vain. Then the tax was extended to the inland counties; Coventry, the Lord Keeper, having obtained an opinion from the judges that the demand was legal, and that the occasion of the demand was in the discretion of the king. It is well known that Richard Chambers, who brought an action against the Lord Mayor for imprisoning him on non-payment of the tax, was the first man who had the courage to resist it and suffer for his resistance; and that the famous case of Hampden put an end for a time to the question, till the impost was declared illegal by the Long

Parliament, one of the earliest acts of which was to annul the judgment obtained against Hampden and others. It would be an error to believe, because Hampden's quota was small, that the tax was light. In fact, it was very heavy.

We learn from Laud's journal that his innovations in Church and State provoked immediate hostility. Thus as early as 1627 he tells us that the Dean of Canterbury had stated, 'that there must be a Parliament, and that some must be sacrificed, and that Laud was as like as any.' That on this he went to the king, who said, ' Let me desire you not to trouble yourself with any respects, till you see me forsaking other friends.' So he was complained of in the House of Commons in June, 1628, for licensing Dr. Manwaring's silly sermon. It was characteristic of Charles's contempt for public opinion, that while the House was offended at Laud's conduct, and was inquiring into it, the king instantly made him Bishop of London, for the express purpose of employing such judicial powers as a bishop possessed against the Puritans, whose stronghold was the city. Laud was elected Bishop of London on July 1, 1628.

Just after this crisis, on August 23, 1628, Buckingham was assassinated at Portsmouth. Felton, the murderer, was carried to London and examined by the Privy Council. Laud, who was present, pressed him to disclose his accomplices. He denied that he had acted in concert with any one; on which

Laud threatened him with the rack. Felton admitted that torture might wring names from him, and hinted that one of the first which he should probably give would be that of Laud himself. A desperate retort of a desperate man, but one which not a few, who foresaw that Laud longed to be, and would be now chief minister, took note of. The king consulted the judges as to whether he might employ torture to constrain confession. The judges, however, unanimously replied that torture was unknown to the Law of England. They forgot the *peine forte et dure*. But their answer gave occasion to the saying, that in those days 'Crown law was more favourable to the subject than Crown divinity.' The judges had no liking for the ecclesiastics, and did not care to be identified with them. 'Let us,' said one of them on a subsequent occasion, 'bail this man, for they begin to say in the town that the judges have overthrown the Law, and the bishops the Gospel.' Laud's life was threatened in anonymous letters and placards. These papers called him from time to time 'the fountain of all wickedness, the arch-wolf of Canterbury, who persecuted the lambs, and shed the blood of martyrs;' asserted that 'the devil was his landlord, and that the government of the Church is a candle in the snuff, going out in a stench.'

On April 10, 1630, the Earl of Pembroke, Chancellor of the University of Oxford, died, and Laud was instantly, i. e. two days afterwards, elected in his room. The election, according to Antony Wood, was not effected without suspicion of foul play, for it was asserted at the time that the majority of the suffrages was given for the Earl of Montgomery, Pembroke's younger brother, and that the Senior Proctor, being a partisan of Laud, gave a false return on the scrutiny.

It is the custom of the great English Universities to set at the head of their affairs some leading statesman, who reflects in the most marked manner the political sentiments of the majority, or at least of those who intrigue with the majority. The tendency of Cambridge has been generally liberal, though this University affects royal personages. It was with great difficulty, and only under pressure, that the Duke of Buckingham, Laud's patron, was elected by the Cambridge masters. Oxford, on the other hand, has generally reflected through her Chancellor the narrowest bigotry of her clergy, that uncompromising hatred of civil and religious liberty which the ecclesiastics of the Establishment have usually and unhappily exhibited. They seated the advocates of prerogative in the times of the Stuarts; Jacobites as long as Jacobites lasted; and the most reactionary politicians since. This disposition to endorse the reputation of the narrowest statesmen is undoubtedly stimulated by the unfortunate accident that the Universities have been supplied with a political suffrage.

The privilege of representation in Parliament, which Elizabeth constantly and prudently refused to the Universities of Oxford and Cambridge, James as unwisely conferred on them. It has been a pernicious boon, the bestowal of which had no defence at the time, which has no defence now, except on that anarchical and degrading theory of representation which would fill Parliament with the nominees of professions, trades-unions, voluntary associations, and the like. No person who has any knowledge of human nature would doubt that the representative of a particular caste or class, or calling, elected by such a body, must be nothing but the delegate of the lowest and most general interests of the class in question, and must discredit a higher and more generous intelligence by even appearing to represent it. If the Bar sent its members as a corporation, it would be represented by the nominees of the scum and dregs of the legal profession. If Medicine were similarly represented, the interests which such members would be instructed to serve would be the most sordid imaginable. But it is almost unnecessary to dwell on this topic when we have before us an experience, extended over two centuries and a half, of academical representation. Oxford sent Selden to the Long Parliament: but during the whole of her parliamentary career she has, except on rare occasions, been represented by the most trivial nobodies which the House has contained, and for this most obvious reason—that no man who is other than narrow, bigoted, and reactionary has ever been able to retain a permanent hold on the rank and file of an academical constituency. If better men have occasionally sat for Oxford, the tenure of their seat has been precarious. It was not long ago that an eminent individual declined to stand for a University. It is currently reported that he alleged that no person who had adequate self-respect would sit for such electors. The Universities are the Helots of our representative system; and if they serve no other purpose, are a permanent warning against any further acceptance of a theory which has failed so egregiously, since the case where the best results which the system could have obtained has been so utterly unsatisfactory.

But though the contribution of the Universities to the aggregate wisdom of Parliament has been so contemptible, the effect of turning a great place of education into a parliamentary borough, with the apparatus of electioneering agents, wire-pullers, and political committees, with the thousand and one meannesses which precede and the miserable bitternesses which follow an election, is in the highest degree disastrous, and is certain to create and foster perpetual feuds.

It is no doubt inevitable that some of these abominations should occur under any parliamentary system, because devotion to high interests is parodied by bad men, and vulgar ambition uses base instruments. But a great University should be carefully secluded from such contingencies, lest it forget its true work, and be embroiled in struggles which disturb and degrade it. It does not need the aid of parliamentary representation in order to secure its social position. Its usefulness in exhibiting a high standard of thought, of learning, of self-respect; and in forming a counterpoise in public estimation to the ignorant vulgarity of sudden wealth, and the equally vulgar insolence of hereditary rank, give it dignity enough, and constitute its true social value. It wants independence. But it does not and cannot get this when it becomes a party in political strife. Nor does it require more assistance from the legislature than is needed in order that it may manage its own affairs for the greatest possible public good. It would be far better if it were not represented at all in the House of Commons. But the next best thing is that which has generally happened, that its ablest and most serviceable members should stand aloof from all political action as far as it is concerned, and allow with indifference, what they cannot prevent by action, that the bigotry and ignorance of the many should be allowed free play in this particular. No doubt the privilege of parliamentary representation is imposing to such Universities as have not been gifted with it. It is possible that the foolish wish of making as much show as one's neighbour may influence academical minds. But equality may be effected by the extinction of mischievous privileges, as well as by their extension; and it is certain that educated men cannot commit a greater error than by claiming, or gain a greater evil than by obtaining, sectional representation.

Before he became Chancellor, Laud had interested himself in academical reform. He had contrived an alteration in the method by which the Proctors of the University were elected. He had done something towards reducing the customs and statutes of the University into a code. But when he obtained the post of chief officer in the University, he devoted himself to the details of its government. His correspondence with his deputy was incessant; his attention to events vigilant. He kept himself minutely informed of everything that went on, and required instant obedience to his orders. He gives us in his diary an illustration of how he dealt with what he calls disorders. It appears that certain persons resented his espionage or his authority, as exercised by his deputy, and that the Proctors took the part of the malcontents. The matter was brought before the king. Three of the ringleaders were expelled. The Proctors were deprived of their office, and others elected in their room; and Prideaux, Rector of Exeter College, and Wilkinson, Principal of Magdalen Hall, were sharply reprimanded. Wilkinson was an eminent Puritan, and was subsequently one of Oliver's commissioners for reforming the University. But the three exiles, according to Wood, were afterwards strong royalists.

The principal change, however, which Laud is credited with having introduced into the government of the University, was the bestowal of the initiative in all academical legislation on the heads of Colleges and Halls. He thereby practically conferred the government of the University on these personages. In 1633 the King ordered the University to create such a board by statute, of course under Laud's advice. Up to this time the tradition of the University was, that the Proctors could summon the Masters of Arts, and then propound statutes to them for their debate, acceptance, and rejection. These officials had even the power of convoking the same body, and submitting to it a decree for the deprivation or compulsory abdication of the Chancellor. It was after an act of this kind, done at the instance of the two Proctors, and in despite of Duppa, Laud's Vice-Chancellor, that the king constrained the University to make a fundamental innovation in its constitution.

The consequence of this change was, that the University was absorbed in the Colleges. Soon no person was allowed to study in Oxford, or remain a member of the corporation, except under the condition of being enrolled in some one or the other of these societies. This legislation put an end to the independent members of the University, and by granting a monopoly to certain existing institutions, lowered all motives of diligence on the part of the teachers. And if the teachers were bad, the rulers were worse.

The headship of a college is the best prize which the fellows of the society have to bestow. It rarely involves duties of any but the most ordinary and routine kind; for the fellows being equal, are naturally jealous of the head whom they have to choose, and strive as far as possible to deprive his reign of the functions of government. Nor is the head invariably elected for literary or intellectual qualifications. He frequently owes his elevation to an intrigue, and over and over again notable scandals have attended the process of his election. But though every effort has been made to isolate each Head in the society over which he presides, the Heads were collectively made the governors of the University. It was as though the several European states succeeded in reducing their monarchs to nullities at home, and yet permitted them as a body to exercise absolute authority over the general politics of the whole continent.

In 1633, Laud was made Chancellor of the Irish University. But absolute as he now was over Oxford and Dublin, he was still thwarted in the Colleges at Oxford, which though contained in the University, and by his legislation containing it, were independent corporations, managing their own affairs, and responsible to no one except their Visitor, nor even to him, except on appeal. In 1636, therefore, Laud, on a hearing before the king at Hampton Court, obtained the right as Metropolitan to visit both Universities, and thereupon to supersede or override the functions of the ordinary judges of appeal. The claim, and the grant of the claim, were unquestionable innovations, for it was a fundamental characteristic of the academical franchise that no ecclesiastical authority could control the action of the Universities. But in the days of the High Commission Court, the interference of the bishops in matters of conduct was justified on pleas like those by which the popes arrogated the right of sitting in judgment on all offences. Nor did this plea rust for want of use. So thorough a royalist and churchman as Falkland could say, 'that the English clergy had opposed the papacy beyond the seas, in order that they might settle one beyond the water,' —meaning Lambeth.

The intimacy between Laud and Strafford, then President of the North, and subsequently the king's deputy in Ireland, began, according to the diary, in the early part of 1631. He 'held a conference with the President of the North in his little chamber in London House,' and regularly corresponded with him afterwards. The principle of government on which the Churchman and the Politician agreed was simple enough. They designated it as Thorough. It consisted in the suppression of all right as against the prerogative, and in the exercise of unsparing severity against all opposition. Strafford, to be sure, was incomparably the abler of the two; but with all his abilities he laboured under the defect which characterises every conservative politician, that, namely, of ignorance about the forces arrayed against him. Had he been able to save Charles from the insensate folly of thrusting, at Laud's suggestion, the English Service-book upon the Scotch people, he would still have failed, and in the end have paid for his failure with his head, or at least with forfeiture and banishment. The Puritans were reformers in their way, and they were convinced that no intelligent and well-informed man could support the prerogative, as the courtiers supported it, unless he were privileged or dishonest. They believed that the Church and King theory, which constituted the conservatism of that time, had no foundation except in ignorance and knavery, and they tried to enlighten the one, and to crush the other. Had Strafford remained in England— he was not Strafford till just before his return— he could not have prevented the king's humiliation, but he might have made it much more gradual, and perhaps have even effected a compromise. It is not impracticable for a public man, who begins on the popular and deserts to the privileged side, to act as a mediator between the two parties, and even to do the work of the former, under the pretence of advocating the interests of the latter. But no such person, however much he may strive to keep the present state of things unchanged, will ever, unless he be madman or fool, seek to violently impose on those who repudiate it, that which he can only defend to those who suffer it. It is not unnatural that those who are familiar with existing institutions should insist that they work well, when the public good progresses in spite of them. It is perfectly natural that shrewd politicians should play on the credulity of their dupes by asserting that the opponents of such institutions cherish sinister ends. But there never yet was a statesman who has succeeded in permanently thrusting innovations on a reluctant people; and no wise statesman attempts to do so, because he knows that such an attempt is perfectly certain to fail.

In 1633 the Lord Deputy went to Ireland. He thought, and constantly asserted that he thought himself sent to a subject, but half-conquered country, which it was his business in the interest of the king, and dimly, in that of the English nation, to thoroughly subdue. That he intended to forward the material prosperity of the Anglo-Irish is proved by the patronage which he bestowed on the Irish linen manufactory, an industry which owes its origin to his policy. That he insulted the best of the Irish prelates, and treated haughtily the ancient Anglo-Irish nobility, is well known. He might, it is true, have thought this politic, but his manner seems to have been that of an upstart, who was resolved to excuse his antecedents by invariable self-assertion and hauteur; and of a convert to absolutism, who was determined to blot out the memory of his earlier attachment to liberty, by a rancorous hostility to all liberty and every private right.

There is nothing, perhaps, which strikes the imagination more forcibly, than the fact that, on the first of May 1638, when the Scotch troubles were just at their commencement, a proclamation was issued forbidding any person from emigrating to New England, except under licence of the Crown, and evidence of conformity supplied by the minister of the parish from which the intending emigrant was setting out. The folly of the proclamation was manifest, since the best thing for Charles and Laud, whatever might be said for the country, was the expatriation of such men as Lords Say and Brook, Sir Arthur Haslerig, Hampden, and Cromwell, who had resolved to leave England for America, and were prevented by this proclamation. But in fact, the absence of no man, however prominent he may have been made by events, would have arrested political change, when the elements of strife were such as those which were gathered in Old St. Stephen's in November 1640. No cause fails for lack of leaders; though it may fail by the treachery or cowardice of those in whom the people have put their confidence. Had these men quitted England, the revolution would have made progress, and other names would have been distinguished, while the same or similar events would have happened.

Strafford was recalled to England by the crisis in which the king's affairs were placed by the Scotch outbreak, by the enthusiastic adoption of the Solemn League and Covenant, by the resistance which the Scotch made to Hamilton the king's Commissioner, and by the disasters which the temerity of Laud and the infatuation of Charles had brought upon the country. On October 5, 1639, the king, with infinite unwillingness, resolved on a Parliament. The opposition, though angry and alarmed, was not as yet prepared for extreme measures. Parliament met on April 13, 1640. But the old question must needs be settled first—grievance before supply. The Lords were willing to invert the order. The Commons retorted that certain things must needs be remedied. They were as follows. The violation of privilege in the suspension of Parliament. Innovations in religion. Grievances against the property and goods of the king's subjects. The imprisonment of Eliot and his colleagues. Ship-money. To have granted supply before these questions were determined would have been infatuation. So the king dissolved the Parliament in person on May 5, published a declaration of the reasons which led him to this proceeding, and then, as if to give abundant demonstration that nothing could be expected from him until he was disabled from doing mischief, betook himself to his old practice of sending members to the Tower. It augured ill for the Church, that when the House of Commons was dissolved, the Convocation of the clergy continued to sit, and passed a series of canons for the government of that body whose destruction was imminent. Then came the gathering of peers at York, and the desperate but inevitable expedient of summoning another Parliament.

The handwriting was now on the wall, though there was no Daniel to interpret it. The men who had been dismissed in May, came back in November, prepared for the struggle, and resolved to extort their demands. It is admitted, on all hands, that the first Parliament of 1640 was disposed to be conciliatory. It was proved very speedily that the second would accept no compromise which did not secure public liberty, which did not effect a thorough and permanent reform.

For nearly twelve years these islands were subjected to personal government. The king had chosen his ministers from renegades and adventurers. He had allied himself with political churchmen, whose tenets were detested by the people, whose pretensions were in violent contrast to public liberty. He had taxed his people without their consent, tampered with or oppressed the municipalities, and deported remonstrants, when he dared, to English prisons, though he had not ventured on hurrying them off secretly to the pestilential shores of the tropical West. He had distinguished between 'Parliamentary counsel and Parliamentary control,' between 'liberty and the abuse of liberty,' and assured these counsellors that they were in his power for 'calling, sitting, and dissolution.' He had been exceedingly averse to interpellations, and to the assertion that his ministers were responsible. After dissolving one, he had called another Parliament, and had informed it, that he must 'save that which the follies of some particular men may otherwise hazard to lose;' a sentence which in modern jargon is equivalent to the advice that a Parliament should save liberty, while the ruler is responsible for keeping order. He had bidden his agents interrupt and silence those who interfere with affairs of State. He had held that 'the people's liberties strengthen the king's prerogative,' but had forgotten the liberties in the prerogative. He had charged the Parliament with instigating hatred and contempt against his administration, had mutilated and imprisoned those private individuals whom he thought proper to prosecute. He was dark, uncertain, unteachable; and his wife was a vain, handsome, imperious bigot, who controlled what judgment he had. He was not indeed, even with his flatterers and hirelings, the arbiter of Europe, though he was ambitious of intermeddling in foreign politics. In 1629 he achieved a *coup d'état*, but he met in 1640 a hostile and determined Parliament, which he tried in vain to coerce. And, finally, he had to deal, when he confronted them, with men who preferred conscience and right to every earthly consideration, with men who believed sincerely in their duty to God and man.

Before these resolute and angry men, bent upon taking vengeance for twelve years' misrule and tyranny, and full of stern purpose against the advisers of these wrongs and outrages, Charles was arraigned in the person of his ministers. It was certain that one humiliation after another would be put on the unhappy king, and that the death of Strafford, the imprisonment of Laud, the permanence of Parliament, the abolition of the Star Chamber and the Commission Court, and the guarantee of liberty against arbitrary government, would not satisfy men who had achieved sudden freedom after so long a bondage. It has been said that the first error which the king committed was that of abandoning the right of dissolution. But such a concession was inevitable. Charles gave them what they asked, and they, knowing that there must be a continual struggle, answered with the Remonstrance. A month afterwards, and the king puts an end to all hope of conciliation by attempting the arrest of the five members. Goaded to this act by the queen's passionate reproaches, while his counsels were betrayed by Lady Carlisle, Charles committed the first act of war, and made the quarrel irreconcileable.

Before this, however, Strafford had passed to the scaffold, and Laud to the prison from which, after four years' detention, he also went to his death. It is said that he might have escaped had he tried, but that he preferred to abide his fortune. Whatever were his faults, no one could charge him with want of fortitude. He bore his imprisonment bravely, busied himself in writing an account of his troubles, and seems to have behaved with dignity to those who insulted his old age and misfortunes. He had been an adviser of tyranny, but he had none of that cowardly meanness, that abject craving for forgiveness, which the brutal instruments of oppression exhibit when they are driven to extremities. Laud waited in Lambeth till he was arrested by Parliament, and went to the Tower with gravity and composure. Jeffreys disguised himself as a sailor, and hid himself in a pothouse in Wapping.

The execution of Laud, a man more than seventy years old, who had been in prison more than four years, and who represented a system now utterly beaten down and powerless, was an act of astonishing folly. He may have been as criminal as Strafford, but he had never been an apostate. He may have acquiesced or counselled the misgovernment of the twelve years, but he was one among many counsellors who had sanctioned the same policy. It may have been necessary to put Strafford out of the way, for had he been pardoned after conviction, he would have carried the strongest will and the clearest head into the king's army. Laud was nothing but a powerless old priest, who must after his release have gone into retirement and obscurity. It may be that all punishment is to be interpreted by considerations of expediency. It is certain that all punishment inflicted for political offences should be measured by nothing but expediency, and that in order to obviate reaction, it is above all things necessary that such punishments should be absolutely free from any appearance of vindictiveness. Now it is ridiculous to imagine that Laud's release could have imperilled public liberty. It is equally ridiculous to doubt that his execution was a blunder, committed in order to gratify sectarian bitterness. Could any punishment be greater to Laud, than to witness the absolute and irretrievable downfal of those projects which had been the objects of his life? He wished to extend the king's prerogative. He had helped mightily towards reducing that prerogative to a shadow. He wished to put the Church into the position which it occupied in the Middle Ages, as it was under the rule of Wykeham, Courtenay, Arundel, Beaufort, Morton, as he acknowledges in his diary, when he rejoices over the promotion of Juxon to the office of Lord Treasurer. He lived to see it an outlawed sect, its power annihilated, its hierarchy proscribed, its liturgy abolished.

The Long Parliament made Laud a martyr, and gave occasion to the reaction which canonized him. It excused his faults, it exalted his virtues, it glorified his memory. His perversity destroyed the Church, his violent death revived it. He might have had the reputation of a meddling and intolerant priest, and the Long Parliament did its best to make him a saint. Posterity would have judged him by the ruin which he brought upon the institutions which he strove to foster. But by the ferocity of those who hounded Parliament on to the vote of December 1644, he became one of the few prelates of the Anglican communion who have perished for the Church. The execution of Laud, and his consequent beatification, have been made a precedent for Anglican sacerdotalism, and form an apology for his public career. But a religious, no less than a political, democracy ought never, by the common-sense rule of self-preservation, to imitate the severity of those who identify themselves with privilege.

Lord Clarendon, that shrewdest and meanest of great names, has, in a well-known sentence, commented on the incapacity of clergymen in dealing with public affairs. The passage has been often quoted, in order to justify the exclusion of clergymen from civil rights. But the incapacity is professional, and extends to other occupations as well. I am not aware that wise, temperate, even necessary legislation has ever proceeded in any notable degree from the overwhelming presence of lawyers in the House of Commons. Who would expect any broad and generous interpretation of public questions from protection societies and trades-unions? Such clergymen as now take part in legislation are the avowed representatives of a section, of a special class-interest, and as such invariably reflect the mediocrity of that class-interest. If such personages still were, as they were two or three centuries ago, entrusted with offices of State, they would have the same disposition to interpret public policy as it bears upon the authority of the order with which they are permanently associated. It is probable, since they naturally set so high a store upon the tenets which they inculcate, that they would be more apt than other professional persons to make the material interests of society wait upon the policy of their own order. In the tacit bargain which now holds, under which the privileged classes obtain the services of the Established Church, and the Church claims protection against all those who do not acknowledge her authority as a political institution, one half of the English people is forbidden the best advantages of the highest education, one third of all the children of England is debarred from the benefits of primary teaching. Now such a bargain is as unjust as it is impolitic. It imperils privilege, and discredits religion.

The incapacity on which Clarendon comments is matter of degree, and attaches itself to any profession, order, class, union, association, which strives to vindicate peculiar importance and peculiar privileges to itself. But if it is inexpedient to entrust the general interests of society to the prejudices of a professional instinct or a privileged class, it is equally inexpedient to annex formal disabilities to any calling, order, or profession. It is certain, if society chooses to employ the services or recognise the claims of any class or profession, that it will indirectly compensate those who are disabled. To curtail the civil rights of the clergy is sure to enlist superstitious reverence in their favour; to exclude them from the direct competition of social forces, is sure to encourage them in claiming, and to justify the public in conceding, supernatural or mystical powers in their office.

The legislature excluded Roman Catholics from practice at the Bar. It is said that they became conveyancers, and that we owe to the ingenuity which intolerance perverted, those tortuous subtleties which have made the English law of real property an intolerable nuisance. The legislature has narrowed the civil rights of the clergy; has loaded them with disabilities; and has striven to harden them into a caste. As a consequence, they have arrogated an authority to which Laud and the Anglicans of the seventeenth century would have hardly dared to aspire; and, unless we are grievously misinformed, they are steadily engaged in reversing the Reformation. Perhaps before it is too late, statesmen may learn that, as it is unwise to entrust public interests to professional prejudice, so it is not less mischievous to erect an imperium in imperio, by rigidly defining the energies of an aggressive and restless profession, and debarring it from any other form of public activity.

JOHN WILKES.

K

JOHN HORNE TOOKE.

JOHN HORNE TOOKE.

THERE is no study more wearisome and unprofitable than that of ecclesiastical history. There is no page of ecclesiastical history so wearisome and unprofitable as that which records the facts of the eighteenth century. There is no portion of the page which is so hopelessly wearisome and unprofitable as the ecclesiastical history of England throughout the whole of that epoch. There is nothing which shows how vital are the powers which lie within Christianity, and how incessantly they aid an awakened conscience and enforce social duties, more clearly than the fact that, after the utter darkness of that age, Christianity effected a revival and renewed itself. My hearers will, I hope, recognise that I am speaking of Christianity in its broadest and most inclusive sense. The darkness to which I refer was general, was as characteristic of continental nations as it was of our own people. But although I do not feel myself justified in dealing with any of the facts which have attended the later revival of Christianity, I think I shall be able to show that some of the circumstances which accompanied the public career of the man whose name is the subject of my Lecture, have left a deep impression on the social life of this country, and, through it, on the life of every civilised community. It is perfectly true, as the first philosopher of history averred, that small acts are rather an index of current opinion than a cause of it. But a very small act may become indirectly the beginning of a powerful principle, which may exercise a vast latent influence, and may challenge attention only when it becomes an established motive, influencing the minds and acts of those whom it was never designed originally to affect.

Up to the Reformation the Church of England was rich. From the middle of the fourteenth century many of its benefices and bishoprics were occupied by cadets of the aristocracy. It is said that Henry, afterwards the eighth king of that name, was destined for the Church and the English primacy as long as he was a younger son, and that we owe the interest which this monarch took in ecclesiastical matters to the fact that he escaped this profession, after receiving some training for it, only by the death of his brother Arthur. But on this side of that eventful period in which Henry broke away from the Roman Church, and impropriated so much of the revenues which had formerly belonged to ecclesiastics, the Church was depressed, poor, and uninviting. It is said that between the Reformation and the Revolution only one prelate of noble descent had sat on the bishop's bench. This was Compton, bishop of London, one of the seven who stood their trial in the last year of James the Second, and who made, for a time at least, episcopacy a popular power in Great Britain.

The Revolution was followed by the schism of the Nonjurors in England, the establishment of Presbyterianism in Scotland, and the Penal Code in Ireland. The Nonjurors declined to acknowledge the settlement of the crown on William, Anne, and the Hanoverian family. But their opposition was passive. They suffered loss, but they did not brave persecution. The tenet of passive obedience which enforced their retirement from the State Church, saved them from the temptation of joining in any active measures for the forcible restoration of the Stuarts. But though their dogma made them submissive, the patience which they displayed made them more or less popular. It is a moot question, the decision of which, since the precedents contradict each other, is difficult, whether patient endurance aids in the furtherance of religious opinion more than active combat does. Both have been tried, both have succeeded, both have failed. Illustrations may be gathered from the history of rival creeds, from the history of rival sects, lying within the same general creed. It is doubtful whether the military success of Mohammedanism was more effectual than the zealous endurance of early Christianity; whether the fierce struggle which extirpated Arianism leavened Christianity more than the resolute endurance of the

English Lollards and the early Hussites; whether the loud preaching of the people called Quakers, under the pertinacious activity of Fox, was more influential than the silent preaching of Penn and the gentler sectaries of his organised benevolence.

The dynasty of the Revolution looked with alarm on the Nonjuring party. It could not believe that the doctrines of passive obedience and indefeasible loyalty were compatible with acquiescence in the accomplished facts which accompanied the Revolution. The politicians of that age had not learned that sectaries may be made always liberal and always loyal; that toleration is nearly as good a check to the political partisanship of dissatisfied churchmen as the legal equality of religious sects is; and that the best way in which a State can obviate the hostility of theological malcontents is to shut its ears to any other claim than that of civil liberty, while the worst policy which any government can adopt is that of allying itself with a polemical propaganda. It is only a little less erroneous to believe that concessions of principle to political theologians are guarantees that they, in whose favour the concession is made, will be faithful to the statesman who makes the grant, or that a compromise by which an ecclesiastical faction is gratified will form a barrier which other interests will be unable to surmount. No alliance is so seductive to shallow politicians as that of ecclesiastical authority and civil power, none has been so uniformly disastrous to the best interests of religion and justice. The government of the Revolution entered into a compact with the Church of the day, and thereupon belied those principles of civil liberty on which the Revolution was justified.

It persecuted the Roman Catholics and the Dissenters, by laying civil disabilities on the profession of a religious creed. It assumed that the acceptance of certain tenets was incompatible with the character of a good citizen in a free State. Hence the occasional Conformity Bill, designed to disable the Dissenters, and the various penal statutes put in England on the Roman Catholics. But history proves over and over again that men who differ fundamentally on forms of faith, may be safely trusted with the joint defence of a common country. The English Catholics were as loyal to the Crown during that terrible autumn when the Armada was threatening England as those were who adhered to the established religion. The Puritans of the same time were as willing to lay down their lives in defence of their country as the most devoted admirers of episcopal institutions were, though Elizabeth's administration treated both with the same merciless severity. And similarly the English Catholics gave scanty aid to the last attempt which the House of Stuart made to regain its inheritance, while the English Dissenters were the firm and consistent allies of a government which treated them with so much injustice and harshness.

The policy under which England was governed was adopted in an exaggerated form in Ireland. Here, the bulk of the people were Catholics. It is certain that the eagerness with which the Irish have embraced, and the perseverance with which they have maintained the Roman faith, are due as much to political causes as to religious feeling. The Irish nation, continually reinforced by immigrants whom it has incorporated into itself, has always striven to assert itself against the English. Now a common faith is a powerful bond between those who entertain a common purpose. The vitality of the Irish race is as remarkable a phenomenon as its settled vindictiveness against the British government. There is no parallel to either. But it must also be admitted that history affords no parallel to the policy of the English government from the days of William the Third to those in which the Irish Parliament achieved political independence, and thereupon set about relaxing, Protestant though it was, the atrocious severity of the Penal Code.

There were two colonies in Ireland, on which the English government relied for maintaining its rule over the Irish people; the Scotch settlement in Ulster, and the English of the Established Church. The former of these laboured under disabilities differing in degree only from those which affected the Catholics. Even the latter had only a limited authority. An Act of Henry the Seventh, procured by Deputy Poynings at the Parliament of Drogheda, and known by his name, forbad the Irish legislature from initiating measures without the consent of the English

Privy Council, and gave the force of law in Ireland to all statutes enacted by English Parliaments up to that date. Two packed Parliaments in the reigns of Henry the Eighth and Elizabeth had forced the Reformation on the Irish people, and the real government of Ireland between the years 1726 and 1764 was put into the hands of the three Primates, Boulter, Hoadley, and Stone, who continuously held the title of Lord Justice.

The Penal Code was designed to exterminate the Irish people. Papists were disabled from keeping schools, in order to prevent the education of priests, and a foreign education was prohibited under the severest penalties, the burden of proof being laid on the accused person, and the decision on the fact being taken from the juries and conferred on the justices at quarter sessions. Intermarriages between Papists and Protestants were forbidden, and if a Protestant married a Catholic woman, he lost his civil rights. Papists were disabled from purchasing greater interests in land than a lease for twenty-one years. If a Papist succeeded to any estate by descent, devise, or settlement, he was to conform within six months, on pain of forfeiture to the next Protestant heir. If the son turned Protestant, he could at once reduce his Catholic father to the condition of a tenant for life. It is almost superfluous to say that the use of arms was denied to Papists, and search might be made for them at any time by two justices. As a whimsical corollary of this law, no Papist was allowed to be a gamekeeper. But these and similar statutes, though they effected one end, that of the transference to Protestant owners of such land as had not already been forfeited and granted to English settlers, failed to make any lasting impression on the national faith and national aspirations of the Irish people. And when in 1782 the Protestant Parliament in Ireland repealed some of these statutes, Sir Hercules Langrishe, a warm advocate of more generous measures, rested his plea on gounds of public and private policy. 'By allowing,' he said, 'Roman Catholics to possess the fee of lands, you for ever bar the claim of old proprietors,'—i. e. of those who had been dispossessed by successive confiscations,—' and interest every Catholic who enjoys such possessions on behalf of the established government.'

In England therefore, and still more in Ireland, the Established Church was taken under the protection and into the confidence of government. As a consequence, and apart from any direct understanding between the heads of the Church and the statesmen who selected and employed them, the Anglican Church adopted Latitudinarian and Erastian views in necessary opposition to those which were characteristic of the Nonjurors and the Dissenters. The former retained much of the traditions of the Laudian epoch, coupling their theories of non-resistance and Divine right with the cognate tenet of extreme sacerdotalism. The latter affected great precision of manner, and insisted on strict discipline and decorum.

The clergy of the Establishment repudiated sacerdotalism, and showed their disdain for the prim manners and severe propriety of the Nonconformists. For a time, indeed, the inferior clergy generally affected a sympathy with the tenets of the older generation of divines. But the school of High Churchmen, whose opinions had gained so unnecessary a notoriety in consequence of the ill-judged trial of Sacheverel, and which had been caressed by Bolingbroke and the Jacobites of Queen Anne's time, was annihilated by the banishment of Bolingbroke, by the suppression of Convocation, and by the issue of the Bangorian controversy. Under the administration of Walpole, the English Church became thoroughly latitudinarian. In 1763, Lord Strange, eldest son of Lord Derby, the member of Parliament who moved the expulsion of Wilkes six years afterwards, tried to induce the House of Commons to abolish the fast held on the 30th of January. Lord Strange was an opponent of the court. Walpole, who relates the fact, laughs at the absurdity of commemorating the martyrdom of Charles. Half a century before, the motion would have been thought treasonable.

The laxity of conduct, and the languor of belief, which characterised the Anglican Church, pervaded all society. The age became generally sceptical or indifferent. The leaders of thought and action scoffed at all enthusiasm. Hartley and Hume in Scotland, Voltaire in France, were only the most prominent teachers of a pervading opinion. The encyclopædists,

Paley, and the Eclectics were, notwithstanding their differences, the outcome of an age which looked on all religious energy with suspicion or contempt. The indifference of the time extended itself to all churches. It is during this period that many descendants of the English and American Puritans effected an Unitarian secession, that the orthodoxy of the Scotch Presbyterians was not free from the suspicion of laxity in belief, that the Lutheranism of Germany began to include the party of Rationalism, that the Gallican Church was affected by the tone of thought which prevailed in France, and that Rome herself fell into an unaccustomed lethargy. The only reaction against this general negligence of religious belief, was in the efforts of sectaries like Wesley and Whitfield, on whom the politicians and clergy of England looked with unmixed contempt, and in the mysticism of Swedenborg, which attracted little attention in so materialistic and utilitarian an age. The clergy of a community are, as a rule, quite as much affected by the tone of thought which pervades society as the laity is by their teaching. It is only when ecclesiastics are driven or encouraged to employ professional expedients that they constitute themselves a caste. They did so in the twelfth century, when they were the citadel of human right against rapine and violence. But they may follow the same policy with wholly different consequences, if a legislature commits the folly of secluding their interests from those of the general community. They will certainly, if they are visited by a professional disability in any free country, exact a tenfold compensation for the injury, by claiming the fullest privileges of sacerdotalism, and constituting themselves the champions of reaction.

The great mass of the English clergy was miserably poor. The law forbad pluralities, but the King and Archbishop could grant a dispensation enabling the favourites of either, or the favourites of their favourites, to hold as many benefices as fortune conferred on well-connected clergymen. Besides, a large number of livings were then, as now, in the gift of private patrons, and it was a common custom for patrons to enter into an arrangement with a clergyman, whereby the greater part of the endowment of the parish was appropriated by the patron, the clergyman accepting a portion not much in excess of the stipend of an ordinary curate. This custom, once very general, is in all likelihood not extinct now, especially in places where public opinion speaks feebly, and the practice may be kept secret.

Contemporary novels are good evidence of manners, and the novels of the eighteenth century enable us to reproduce the parson of the time with ease. He generally appeared in public in gown, cassock, and bands; not because custom prescribed a costume in his case only, but because most men who plied a profession were habited in official dress. The barrister was as regularly robed as the parson. The physician was similarly known by his formal wig and equally formal staff. In fact, a century ago, a man's dress designated his rank and calling. He was licensed to carry on a particular occupation, and he advertised his occupation accordingly, especially as no small part of his income was derived from the fees for which he competed. Thus, before Lord Hardwicke's Marriage Act, a particular class of clergymen, not, it may be imagined, in very good repute, touted for marriage-fees as some low attorneys do for practice. The Act I have referred to, while it still required the office of some legally-ordained clergyman in order to give validity to the marriage, demanded publicity before and at marriage, or licence before and publicity at marriage, and furthermore ordained that the marriage-service should be read in a church. One Keith, who made a handsome income by solemnising clandestine marriages in Mayfair, and who was deprived of his trade by the Act, threatened that he would open a graveyard and bury, in opposition to the beneficed clergy and the bishops. His threat has been carried out by others in later times. But in the days of Keith, the practice of compensating influential persons, in order to obtain their acquiescence in the abolition of abuses, was inchoate. The Church, in short, was a profession whose practitioners were sometimes fortunate enough to secure certain prizes, while the rank and file performed offices for the fulfilment of which the law required a particular qualification, and for employment in which men competed, sometimes in particular places, sometimes by wandering over a kind of clerical circuit. There is a story in the Life of Wesley of a conversation between the preacher and an itinerant parson, who complained that he could get only half a guinea for a service. The story is told, not to shew that such Bohemians were scarce, but in order to introduce a theological pun of Wesley's, and the moral which he appended to it.

John Horne, who assumed the name of Tooke when he reached middle life, and is therefore generally known as Horne Tooke, was the third son of John Horne, a prosperous poulterer in Newport Market. He was born on January 25, 1736, in Newport Street, Westminster, and christened the next day at St. Ann's, Soho. Benjamin, the eldest son of this Horne, was a market gardener at Brentford, who attained opulence in his calling by his skill and spirit. The second son, Thomas, was unfortunate, and ended his days in the Fishmongers' Almshouses. Of his two sisters, one married a Mr. Wildman, a friend of Wilkes, the second Dr. Demainbray, who assisted in George the Third's education, and whose son was for many years head of the Kew Observatory. Horne, the father, must have been a man of some consideration, for he was the first treasurer of the Middlesex hospital. In those days, Newport Market was in the outskirts of London.

The boy was first sent to an academy in Soho Square, and thence, in 1744, to Westminster. In 1746, he was transferred to Eton, whose head-master was then Dr. Sumner, where he remained for five or six years. He is said to have made little progress at Eton; but then, as for many a year afterwards, boys got anything except learning at that celebrated school, unless they were at the pains to instruct themselves. At Eton, however, he lost the sight of an eye, from a wound inflicted on him by another boy's penknife.

John Horne, so his mother's friends said, never was a boy. When ten years of age, and therefore just before he went to Eton, he was sent for a short time to a school in Kent. Here he soon ran away, and, to avoid capture, climbed up a chimney. When his pursuers gave up the search, he started for London. Benighted and wet through, he was taken into the house of a peasant, and slept there for the night. Then he got into a cart to go home, where, as he hid himself in the straw, he heard himself described as a wicked little boy with a cast in his eye, who had run away. Many years afterwards, and when his fortunes were at the lowest, he paid the peasant's widow, who had fallen on evil days and poverty, an annuity of £10 a year. And when he reached his home, he excused himself for running away by telling his father that the master was not fit to instruct him, for he might, perhaps, know nouns and adverbs, but nothing of prepositions and conjunctions. At Eton afterwards, he used to tell the boys who bragged of their fathers, that his was an eminent Turkey merchant.

For a time after he left Eton, John Horne was with a private tutor at Sevenoaks, and subsequently with another at Ravenstone. Then he went to St. John's College, Cambridge, from whence he took his Bachelor's degree in 1758. Meanwhile he entered at the Inner Temple, in order to keep his terms for a call to the Bar, a profession to which he always inclined. His companions were Dunning and Kenyon, both afterwards ennobled for eminence in their profession. 'We used,' said Horne, 'to dine in Chancery Lane for sevenpence-halfpenny each. Dunning and I were generous, and gave the girl who waited a penny; but Kenyon, who knew the value of money, sometimes indeed gave her a halfpenny, but more frequently a promise.' Dunning and Kenyon retained these several characteristics in later life.

But Horne the father, who was fond and proud of his son, would not hear of his following the profession of the law. He had set his heart on seeing his son a clergyman; and, apart from any respect he might have entertained for that profession, he had certain private motives for insisting on his authority with his son.

His premises abutted on Leicester House, where Prince Frederic lived. The servants of Frederic's household made a way through these premises, in order to save themselves time and trouble. Horne resented the trespass, remonstrated, and, finding his remonstrances fruitless, brought his action at Westminster. Of course he gained it. He then, however, wrote to the prince, apologised for the necessity he was under of defending his property, and surrendered the right of passage. The prince was pleased, and made him poulterer to his household. Horne got nothing but glory by this appointment, for the prince died several thousand pounds in debt to him; and George the Second, who loved money more than anything besides, took no thought of his son's debts. It is probable that Horne was considerably impoverished by this unlucky patronage, and that the son's prospects were materially injured by the prince's custom.

But he had another motive. One of his daughters had married Dr. Demainbray, who held an office in the prince's household, and was therefore in continual intercourse with the prince. John Horne was the constant playmate of Prince George, who was exactly two years younger than his companion. What more natural than to believe that the losses which the father had suffered, and the youthful intimacy which had existed between the son and the future king, would be compensated and acknowledged in time to come by the exercise of royal patronage? In those days, promotion in the Anglican Church was, and perhaps it still is, an affair of the backstairs.

His father bought him the living of New Brentford, and he reluctantly took priests' orders in 1760. He had been a deacon some time before. The living was worth from £200 to £300 a year, and Horne seems to have set to work honestly in his parish;

to have preached to his parishioners in the strain of the time (for a sermon of his on the moral obligations of Christianity is published); to have avoided all dogmatic theology, except in so far as he thought it proper to expose the pretensions of popery; and to have expressed himself with the contempt which was customary at the time against dissenters and methodists. He was, in short, a Whig latitudinarian clergyman of the Hoadley and Secker school, who might have filled the place which they had with better right, and whose character was incomparably higher than that of Blackburn and Warburton, the former of whom had been a buccaneer (though he retained no part of his old profession but his seraglio), while the latter was infinitely more orthodox in public and in the press than in private and in conversation. As an illustration of Horne's unvarying benevolence and kindness of character, it should be said that he studied physic diligently (there was need of such study at that time), in order to be of service to his poorer parishioners.

But Horne had strong convictions, great kindliness of nature, and nourished an earnest hatred against all oppression. He might have learned the principles of civil liberty in Leicester House, where they were promulgated with infinite readiness, to be repudiated of course afterwards, in the same way as the last George, Prince of Wales, forgot his liberalism when he achieved the regency. Shrewd men are not of course taken in by the professions which are made by expectant monarchs, or by expectant ministers either. 'You don't like princes,' said Frederic to Pope, in one of his interviews with the poet. 'I beg your pardon.' 'Well, you don't like kings.' 'I own that I like the lion best before his claws are grown.' There is in nature no person so amiable as a statesman who seeks to gratify his ambition. There is none, as a rule, less amiable, when that ambition is sated by success.

Horne would have, I make no doubt, remained a quiet and decorous clergyman, if there had been no such persons as Bute and the king's friends, or if Pitt had remained in office. He conceived, in common with most Englishmen, the strongest animosity against Lords Bute and Mansfield, whom he attacked in a mock petition under the names of Lords Mortimer and Jeffreys. He intended, I fear, to glance at the Princess and Pitt, when he said, 'Let Fulvia with her bodkin again pierce through the tongue of Cicero,' and concluded, 'I who am at present blessed with peace, with happiness, with independence, a fair character, and an easy fortune, am at this moment forfeiting them all.' Dr. Demainbray urged him to abstain from publishing so energetic a libel, containing too a prophecy which was so likely to fulfil itself. But Horne never shirked the avowal of his opinions. In a time when anonymous attacks on public characters were the rule, Horne either published his name at the end of his letters, or left regular instructions to his printer to communicate his authorship to anyone who felt himself aggrieved and might inquire for his assailant.

Horne threw himself with all his energy into the cause of Wilkes after the affair of the General Warrant. Like many clergymen of the time, he had gone on a tour in France with young Elwes, the son of the miser, in 1763; and again in 1765, when he undertook a similar engagement with a son of Mr. Taylor. On the latter occasion he was introduced to Wilkes at Paris, who was charmed with his admirer, and exacted on his leaving him a promise that he would correspond with him. Thence he journeyed to Geneva, where he met Voltaire, of whom, by the way, he always expressed a mean opinion, as might have been expected from his straightforward sincerity, then resided some months at Genoa, and returning, spent some weeks at Montpelier, at that time a favourite winter residence with Englishmen. Here he met Adam Smith, who was similarly engaged as travelling tutor to the Duke of Buccleugh. He now bethought himself of his promise to correspond with Wilkes, and sent him a letter, which afterwards had a most sinister effect on his career.

Horne was not yet thirty years old. He was as I have said a political enthusiast, and he entertained a sincere admiration of Wilkes. He believed him to be, not what the world now admits him, an unscrupulous adventurer, whom accident made conspicuous or popular, but a man who had fought manfully on behalf of liberty against oppression. Churchill, who, like Horne, was a clergyman, but who had resigned his office, had a similar admiration for Wilkes. But he would, if he had lived long enough, have detected the worthlessness of his hero, and would have repudiated him as utterly as Horne did, when the disguise was stripped off. There were perhaps good and wise men in ancient Egypt, who worshipped cats, monkeys, and crocodiles, because they were deemed symbols of something good and noble, or because they saw nothing better to worship.

Horne knew that Wilkes was a man of pleasure, a wit, a debauchee, a scoffer at things reputed holy. He had learnt that he was, through the agency of Fitzherbert, receiving £1000 a year from Rockingham, on condition that he remained in Paris. He wished to recall him to a sense of his duty to his country, and happily applied the story of Eutrapelus in Horace to his hero; that Eutrapelus, who, when he wished to extinguish an honest opponent, presented him with fine clothes, and the garniture of luxury, so as to induce him to take the first step to the ruin of character and fortune. And in order to gild the pill of advice, he jested on his own office and profession, spoke of his not being ordained a hypocrite, of the infectious hands of a bishop, of the sop given to Judas, and its resemblance to an every-day ordination, and of the black spot under the tongue of a priest.

Now all this was grossly indecent and unbecoming. If Horne believed what he said, if he meant his words seriously, Wilkes was the last man to whom he should have been so outspoken, because Wilkes was never serious. If, on the contrary, writing to a man considerably older than himself, whom he exceedingly admired, but whom he believed to be neglecting a public duty in sloth and frivolity, and who, as he heard, was taking a minister's pay in order to delay that duty, he wished to affect the thorough man of the world, and to abjure in such company, and while he held communication with such a person, his clerical character, by way of disarming Wilkes, and obviating some retort on his profession, he showed as little courage as he did judgment. Still something must be said for the coarseness of the age. A clergyman in these times, who wrote in such a fashion, would be interpreted to have abjured his relations with the Church, and to have abjured them indecently. In those days, the language of this letter might have shocked some, and would have amused many. Even when the letter was published, Walpole, speaking of him, said that 'no reproach was cast on the morals of Horne, but that to please Wilkes he had ridiculed his lords the bishops, and to please himself, had indulged in more foppery than became his profession.' The letter, too, was not intended for the public.

Wilkes did not make any answer to this letter, and Horne became uneasy. Soon after, he waited on his friend at Paris, and inquired about the Montpelier communication. Wilkes assured him that he had never received it, and affected wonder at the miscarriage. But he had it in his possession, and had shown it to many of his acquaintance. Horne at last felt reassured. During the time that he travelled on the Continent he had dressed like a layman, and on quitting Paris, he left his clothes with Wilkes. The inventory justifies Walpole's comment on his foppery abroad, for we read of scarlet and gold, white and silver, blue and silver, silk and velvet attire. Five years afterwards, when the friends quarrelled irreconcileably, Wilkes published the letter and the inventory. Neither bore upon the dispute. But Horne proved to the world that Wilkes, who complained so bitterly that his papers had been rifled under the general warrant, and that he had suffered in consequence, was a liar and a knave; besides being a traitor to the unwritten law of honour and good faith.

Meanwhile, Horne settled at Brentford, and became a popular preacher, much sought after for city sermons. Then, in 1768, came the Middlesex elections, and the repeated return of Wilkes, and the violent popular excitement. Horne threw himself into the cause with his customary ardour and energy. He canvassed unremittingly. He exclaimed, as he grew warm over the work, that in a cause so just and holy he could dye his black cloth red. When they quarrelled, Wilkes, on whose behalf he had uttered this piece of electioneering gasconade, remembered it, and reproached him with it. Wilkes, who reaped the advantage of Horne's exertions, affected to consider him a bravo, and compared him to orator Henley. But there was nothing which rivalled the effrontery of that man, except his baseness. During the contest, Horne saved Luttrell from the fury of the mob, and after the constituency finally succumbed to the votes of the House of Commons, he favoured the election of Glynne.

Horne had an extraordinary acquaintance with English law, and the following year gave him more than one opportunity of using his knowledge. One Bigby had been murdered, under the most atrocious circumstances, by two brothers, named Kennedy. The men were notoriously dissolute bullies. Their guilt was plain, and conviction followed as a matter of course on their trial. Everybody expected that they would be hung, and nobody doubted the propriety of the execution. But they had a sister, a very conspicuous person, who was then living under the protection of a nobleman. Through her intercession, and by the nobleman's influence, the king was induced to grant a pardon to the ruffians. Horne only expressed the general indignation of the public when he denounced this abominable scandal. But he also hunted up a remedy.

By the ancient English law, a law confirmed by the Great Charter and several statutes, all notable private wrongs could be prosecuted as injuries, under the form of an Appeal. This right was doubtlessly derived from that time, in which a pecuniary compensation was accorded to the injured person, according to a certain schedule of payments for injuries. After the time in which offences were punished as breaches of the king's peace, or felonies against the dignity of the Crown, this right of prosecution was still retained. The reason is obvious. The remedy enabled those who were weak to challenge the greatest by the legal process of appeal; for it is worth noting, as indicating that such was the motive for maintaining the custom, that in case an appeal was prosecuted against a peer of Parliament, he had no privilege, but was constrained to undergo his trial before a common jury. The effect of a verdict on an appeal was the same as in that on an indictment. But since the statutes which upheld this right provided that in case the appeal failed, the appellant should be liable to a year's imprisonment, to a fine, and to an action for damages, the remedy had long been disused, and an ordinary criminal prosecution was found more convenient, and, in general, equally efficacious.

The right of appeal of blood, that is, of prosecuting the offender, was limited to the widow or eldest male heir of the person murdered, or, in case widow or heir were disqualified, or suspected of the offence, to the next male heir. But as the process was the vindication of a private right, the king could no more grant a pardon to a person convicted than he could remit damages given by a jury in a civil action. It was allowed, too, that a conviction or acquittal under an indictment did not do away with the right of appeal.

Upon this law Horne seized. He persuaded the widow to claim this right against the brothers Kennedy, with the certainty that either the pardon must be revoked, or that an enormous scandal would be revealed and exposed. The Court was in consternation; for though, beyond doubt, the king had been imposed on, and was blameless, persons about him would be seriously compromised by the disclosure of the facts. An escape was found. The same noble personage interposed his good offices by his agent. The widow Bigby was, after all, an Ephesian matron. For 350 guineas — which she prudently required should be paid in gold, she consented to waive her appeal. The merciless priest, as Walpole calls him, was baffled, and the brothers escaped.

It appears that political activity is like dram drinking—a passion which cannot be indulged in without great risk of becoming an inveterate habit. In the same year Horne was made a freeman of the town of Bedford, in order to strengthen an opposition to the Duke of Bedford, 'then,' as Junius said, 'the little tyrant of a little corporation.' My hearers will remember the odious picture which Junius draws of the duke. Horne, thus introduced to the franchise, beat the duke on his own ground. In the same year he interposed on behalf of two Spitalfields' weavers, who were convicted and sentenced by Recorder Eyre. The recorder, after giving sentence, had changed the record, and Horne argued that the sentence was wholly vitiated by the alteration. His objection, though fortified by the opinion of Glynne, was overruled.

In the same year he charged Onslow, one of the Lords of the Treasury, in the Public Advertiser, with having taken a bribe of £1000 to procure a Mr. Burns a place in America. Onslow, who had already been in communication with Burns, and was then engaged in trying to detect the persons who had cheated the man (for it is clear that Burns had paid £1000 to somebody in the Treasury), answered indignantly that the statement was false. Horne replied, writing as before under the name of a freeholder of Surrey, that the reply did not clear away the accumulated suspicions which surrounded the transaction. Onslow demanded the author's name, which, as usual, Horne had empowered the printer to communicate, and commenced a civil action for libel. The first trial was held at Kingston, and ended in a nonsuit, owing to some technical flaw. At a second trial in the King's Bench, Onslow obtained a verdict with £400 damages. Horne was resolute, and appealed to the twelve judges, who set aside the verdict. Almost everybody at the time thought Horne to blame. It is certain that many great people were interested in preventing the ventilation of such scandals.

In the same year, Horne, in conjunction with certain wealthy men in the city, founded the society of the Bill of Rights. The original members of this society, fourteen in number, among whom were two clergymen, passed certain resolutions, which are highly praised by Junius. The objects of the society were to support the Liberal press, to accept Wilkes as their champion, and to pay his debts, and to resist any unconstitutional practice; such, for example, as the attempt of Lord Mansfield to convict Bingley, by interrogating him, and by committing him for contempt on his refusal to criminate himself.

But the culminating act of Horne's audacity or courage, was the part he took in the memorable interviews between the king and the corporation of London in 1770. The corporation, according to the ancient privilege of the city, claimed and obtained an audience with the king, in which they petitioned strongly against the ministry and the policy of the Court. The king said that the petition was disrespectful to him, injurious to Parliament, and inconsistent with the principles of the constitution. When the corporation withdrew, the king, as Horne averred, burst out laughing; 'just,' he adds, 'as Nero fiddled when Rome was burning.' Soon after, the corporation prepared a new address and remembrance. The king rebuked the petitioners; and the Lord Mayor, Beckford, who had anticipated the rejoinder, replied with the memorable speech which is engraved on the pedestal of his statue in the Guildhall. Both remonstrance and reply were composed by Horne.

He was now in the height of his popularity. But

he was detested by the Court. He was equally disliked by the aristocracy. Even Walpole, who recognised the services of Wilkes, speaks of him as among the rabble of Wilkes's agents, as a man of slender parts. He must have known that he was doing Horne's abilities injustice; and that a man who was only second to Wilkes in influence, and vastly his superior in character, could not have reached so rapid a reputation as a writer and speaker without great capacity. Of course, however, the king's friends hated him most. They believed, probably, though the terms of the adage have been invented in our time only, that 'a good Churchman must needs be a Conservative,' and that if he be the latter, he may retain the former reputation, even though he ceases to be anything but a nominal Christian. Had Horne employed his talents and energy on the side of the Court and of its policy, he would probably, however vehemently he might have spoken and acted, have become a successor of the Warburtons and the Hayters, or have swollen into the greatness of an Irish primate. It is astonishing, if one did not reflect on the conservative forces of society, to see how fully vituperation, calumny, falsehood, and treachery may be pardoned and rewarded in the partisans of established facts and inveterate abuses.

In January 1771, Horne quarrelled with Wilkes. The real cause of the quarrel was the conduct of the latter, and his attempt to make the society, which was intended to generally serve certain public purposes, a mere agency for collecting money with which to pay the patriot's debts, and to supply him with the material for extravagance and debauchery. The controversy, which was carried out with great bitterness on the part of both, and with amazing turpitude on the part of Wilkes, cost Horne much of his popularity, and augmented that of his opponent. But to us, despite the publication of the Montpelier letter, and the catalogue of the smart unclerical suits, Horne was honest, Wilkes a sordid and perfidious knave. Soon afterwards, Horne was attacked by Junius, and was certainly the victor in the struggle with that mysterious and malignant writer. Years afterwards, Tooke averred that he knew who Junius was. He might have believed it was Temple, of whom Walpole said, 'that he was the familiar of Wilkes and his friends;' and adds, perhaps with the same suspicion, 'that he gave these people secret information, and so enjoyed what he preferred to power; vengeance, and a whole skin.' This Temple died in 1779, and was succeeded in his estates by his nephew. The son of this nephew afterwards attacked Horne's seat when he was returned to the House of Commons. His son was the Protectionist Duke of Bukingham, who speculated in land, and jobbed certain memoirs. But Walter Boyd, to revert to that endless question as to who was Junius, told Alexander Stephens, in the presence of the Governor-General of India, who was, says Stephens, a scholar and a man of letters, that the correspondence was not the work of one man, but of many, and that he (Walter Boyd) was the confidential editor.

In the same year, Horne went to Cambridge to take his Master's degree. He did not get it as a matter of course. His grace was opposed by the well-known Dr. Paley, who himself failed, through suspicion of political heterodoxy, to obtain the preferments which he longed for. Horne was probably a good mark to aim at by a man who was ambitious, and whose prospects seemed dilatory. For however much Walpole and the world might have laughed at the Montpelier letter, the expectants were officially indignant, the Court detested Horne, and the Wilkites, to whom Wilkes did not belong, were ready at their nominal leader's bidding to stone him. George III, his old playfellow in Leicester House, had probably forgotten him and the garden, and the surreptitious way which led to the old poulterer's larder, as his grandfather and he had forgotten Frederic's bad debts—into an infinity of forgetfulness.

Horne now resolved to quit his present profession, and return to that which he had originally designed to enter. In 1772, four of his friends offered him their joint bonds for the payment of £400 a year, till such time as he should be called. He accepted the offer, but he never drew a sixpence from them. In 1773, he resigned Brentford, believing, as everybody probably at that time but a few mystics did, that this act, and the avowal that he forthwith intended to live as a layman, would sever him from all connection with the clerical profession. He now reduced his expenditure to the lowest possible amount, since his resources were considerably diminished. In the step which he took, he was strongly advised by his friend William Tooke, who had been associated with him in the Society of the Bill of Rights, and who, in company with Sawbridge and Townsend, had quitted that association after Horne's quarrel with Wilkes.

Mr. William Tooke had bought the estate of Purley, near Godstone, once the seat of the arch-regicide Bradshaw, and here became involved in some quarrel with a Mr. De Grey. De Grey, who appears to have had some considerable influence in the House of Commons, contrived to get a Bill of Inclosure, which would have annihilated Tooke's real or presumed rights, introduced into the House, and rapidly pushed through its stages. In this difficulty, Tooke consulted Horne, who suggested that the progress of the Bill should be arrested by the publication of a libel on the Speaker, and added that he would write it. It was written, Woodfall was summoned to the bar, avowed that the writer was present, and had authorised him to admit the charge. The Speaker was astonished, and exclaimed, 'What have I done that I should provoke the anger of so powerful a writer?' Horne escaped, partly perhaps by the boldness with which he avowed himself, partly because he raised the plea, that since he had quitted his orders, he was wrongly described as a clergyman in the warrant.

To the measures which led to the outbreak of the War of Independence, Horne showed the most energetic hostility. He was profoundly versed in constitutional law, and he argued with the greatest vehemence, that the Stamp Act and the Tea Duty were unconstitutional; that taxation without representation was contrary to the fundamental principles of political liberty, and that the Government and Parliament were wholly in the wrong. Events proved his reasonings to be right; but the Government and the king were obstinate, and Parliament was the hack of both. Horne was soon to be made a martyr to those principles which are now universally acknowledged by civilised communities. No Englishman ever did more service to a just cause, contributed more powerfully to a right interpretation of the American quarrel, or was more scandalously ill-used than this abdicated clergyman.

He had set on foot another Liberal association, under the name of a 'Society for Constitutional Information.' On the occurrence of the first hostilities between Great Britain and her American colonies, he promoted a subscription 'for the widows and children of our American fellow-subjects, who had been murdered at Lexington and Concord by the king's soldiers, on April 19, 1775,' and in pursuance of this end he paid £100 to Franklin. The Government resolved to treat this as a seditious libel, and Thurlow, then Attorney-General, who afterwards called the Duke of Grafton 'the accident of an accident,' was directed to prosecute him and three newspaper proprietors, who had printed the facts. The newspaper folks pleaded guilty, and were let off with a fine of £100 each.

On June 27, 1776, Horne waited on Thurlow, informed him that he did not mean to pay for a copy of the proceedings, insisted on their being read to him, and said that he should conduct his own case. It came on before Mansfield on July 4, 1779, at Guildhall. Horne demanded that the jury should be taken by ballot. Wilkes sat, enjoying the scene, on the bench, by Mansfield. Horne was convicted, fined £200, imprisoned for a year, and constrained to find securities for three years. Never was a more unrighteous verdict, a more unjust sentence. He appealed in 1778, by writs of error, and employed his friend Dunning as counsel. He appealed however in vain.

He was confined in the King's Bench prison, but, on the payment of a sum of money, he was allowed to occupy a small house within the rules. Here he was regularly visited by his friends, and commenced those philological studies, which he afterwards collected and published in his celebrated 'Diversions of Purley.' Here too he caught the gout, a disorder which he believed that he fairly lived out. He estimated the losses of his trial at £1200, a large sum for a man of narrow fortunes and independent spirit.

Released in 1779, he applied for a call to the bar. The Benchers, who exercise a discretionary power of admission, subject to an appeal to the judges, demurred. A little while before, they had rejected Murphy because he had been a comedian. Now they affected to doubt whether Horne were not still a clergyman, a matter with which, as it was a canonical and not a legal question, they had nothing to do. It was notorious that ecclesiastical canons do not bind the laity, and therefore, unless by express provision of law, cannot be enforced by lay tribunals. The only process which could be taken against Horne was in the ecclesiastical courts, and in those days the practice of worrying clergymen in such courts, by associations and subscriptions, had not been begun, and would very probably, had it been begun, have brought down upon the heads of the association the penalties of conspiracy.

Horne stated his claim. He asked whether the injunctions of an ecclesiastical tribunal, directing clerks to abstain from secular employments, were legally binding? whether since the Reformation such a question had ever been raised? whether they would raise it against any other applicant than himself? whether the profession of a clergyman were indelible? whether a clergyman in full orders cannot be secularised? and, lastly, whether he, by giving up his preferment, did not actually become a layman? It is clear that Horne expected an answer to these questions, and that the answer to the first four would be negative, to the last two affirmative. It is certain that Horne was one of the greatest masters of constitutional law in England, and that he could hardly have put these questions had he not been fully convinced that he was indisputably justified in his claim. The Benchers did not attempt to answer him, but negatived his call. It was only however by a casting-vote that this decision was arrived at, that vote having been given by one Bearcroft, who was afterwards Chief-Justice of Chester. Horne declined to appeal to the Judges and Parliament, a course which lay before him, probably because he was of opinion that he should not get a fair hearing from either.

Baffled in his attempt to enter the profession of the law, and having become, by the sale of his living, and by a bequest from his father, in somewhat easier circumstances, he resolved to take to farming. He purchased a small estate at Witton, near Huntingdon. But he soon caught an ague there, and found retirement in such a district little suited to his tastes. He forthwith sold his farm and returned to London.

Pitt was now engaged in planning his scheme for Parliamentary Reform, which Horne espoused in his well-known letter to Dunning. In this letter he opposes Cartwright's scheme of universal suffrage, though he speaks of the Major, the father of modern radicalism, as his virtuous and inestimable friend. Besides Cartwright and Dunning, Horne enjoyed the friendship of Dr. Jebb, Sheridan, Fox, Lord Surrey, Mr. (afterwards Lord) Grey, and the Duke of Richmond. But he subsequently quarrelled with Fox and

Sheridan, and on nearly the same grounds which led to his rupture with Wilkes, their licentiousness and extravagance. Horne never believed that public liberty could be materially aided by rakes and gamblers, and he said as much in his 'Pair of Patriots,' Fox and Pitt, which he published in 1788.

In 1782, he assumed the name of Tooke. He had long been intimate with William Tooke, was always designated by him as his heir, and was now recognised as having that prospect. It is probable that this change was made at William Tooke's instance. In 1786 he published his 'Diversions of Purley,' the first important work on the Philology of the English language. He espoused no side during the trial of Hastings, perhaps the only great public event during his career on which he was neutral. But he held the policy of the Whigs on the India question, invariably spoke with contempt about the Company, its conquests, and its rights, and asserted that all their acquisitions were the property of the Crown, and held during its pleasure. It is possible that Tooke's animosity to the Company's servants was derived from the old days of his hatred to Bute and the Scotch. The Scotch of the last century were, I fear, no gentle and gracious rulers in India. They were also very numerous. Some years ago, a patriotic Scotchman, with no evil intentions, imported some thistle-down into Australia. It soon became such a nuisance, that the Legislature was constrained to pass a law inflicting a fine of £10 on everybody who failed to cut up his thistles. I fear that this modern experience illustrates the Scotch rule in India in the last century.

Pitt dropped his projected Parliamentary Reform, and disappointed his liberal admirers. Hence in 1790, a society was formed for the purpose of furthering this or a larger scheme. It contained the Duke of Richmond's project, and went under the name of the Corresponding Society. The promoter of this society was John Hardy, a Westminster shoemaker, a man of high religious and moral character, as was afterwards proved at his trial. He visited Tooke, who had made just then great exertions to liberate one Gow from slavery in Algiers, and showed him the rules of the society, of which Tooke approved in general terms.

In 1790, he contested Westminster against Fox. The poll, according to the custom of the time, was open for many days, while gross and disreputable expenditure was incurred to such an amount as actually exceeds that of a Westminster election in our day. No one hinted that Tooke was ineligible by reason of his profession. He polled 1700 votes at a cost of £28. Then he petitioned Parliament in vigorous language. He had satirised Fox and Sheridan on the hustings. Fox induced Sheridan to plead his cause, and Tooke told the crowd, that when the quack doctor withdrew, he left as usual his merry Andrew behind him.

The House voted the petition frivolous and vexatious. In 1780, one Alderman Woldridge had stood and failed at the borough of Abingdon. He then petitioned for the seat; but when his petition came on for hearing, he abandoned it, having provided neither counsel, attorney, nor evidence on his case. The petition was voted frivolous and vexatious, and an Act was passed which laid the costs of any petition which was reported to be of this character, on the petitioner. Hence Fox sued Tooke for the taxed costs of his defence, which amounted to £198 2s. 6d., and recovered them.

He now removed to Wimbledon, where he spent the remainder of his life. Liberal as he was, he adhered steadily to the Constitution, limiting reform to such changes as were proved necessary. Thus, when Lord Stanhope, who had assumed principles not far short of Jacobin, presided at a dinner in order to congratulate the French on the destruction of the Bastille, Tooke proposed and with some difficulty carried a resolution, to the effect 'that England had not such an arduous task as France had, but merely a duty to maintain and improve her Constitution.' As I have already said, he had the heartiest contempt for Paine. It is not a little singular that principles are not so hereditary as wisdom is reputed to be. The leaders of the popular party at that time included a Richmond and a Stanhope. Pitt, however, did not prosecute these people but only their followers, and among them Horne, who was so little a follower of Stanhope, that he defined his opinions to be those of a man who was steadily attached to the ancient freedom of his country, as it was practically enjoyed under those honest old gentlemen Georges I. and II.

He was now visited by spies. With one of these, whom he detected, he played a dangerous game. He affected knowledge and mystery, and amused himself with the interest of his simulated friend. The Government, then in its most frantic terror, resolved to act. They seized Hardy by warrant of the Secretary of State. Then they intercepted a letter, written by the Rev. Jeremiah Joyce, tutor to Lord Stanhope's children, and directed to Tooke. It seemed full of tremendous meaning, and ran as follows:—

'DEAR CITIZEN,

'This morning at six o'clock citizen Hardy was taken away, by order from the Secretary of State's office. They seized everything they could lay their hands on. Query, is it possible to get ready by Thursday?—Yours, 'J. JOYCE.'

To the frightened imagination of Pitt's panic-stricken underlings, this note was portentous. It seemed to threaten riot and insurrection. Nobody troubled himself with the question as to what the resources of the society were. On the trial, it was found that its funds amounted to sixty guineas a year. But the Toryism of Pitt's age was utterly cowardly and utterly merciless. It was overpoweringly strong. It could count on a devoted Parliament, on an efficient army, and on all the ignorance, prejudice, and fanaticism of an illiterate and half-starved rabble in the towns, whom it could rouse to riot by its emissaries, and did rouse to riot. It drove the country into war, in order to evade Parliamentary Reform. It now resolved to attack and hang a man, whose whole public career had been notably stainless and patriotic.

Tooke was seized by a warrant of the Secretary of State on May 16, 1794, and sent to Newgate. He was described as a hoary traitor (a title which in after years he used to repeat, and be toasted by, with infinite relish), as the ringleader of a gang of conspirators, as pledged to destroy our glorious constitution in Church and State. It is unnecessary to say that Tooke had no political secrets, that he was in the strictest sense of the word a constitutionalist, even to the verge of pedantry, and that with its innumerable faults and vices, then more gross and scandalous than at any period of its history, he was a firm supporter of the Church Establishment.

It is probable that Tooke's enemies hoped that he would perish in Newgate, where he was confined for several months. The water trickled down the walls of his cell, the bed was damp, the air was unwholesome. But Tooke was a man whose courage and power were equal to every occasion. It is certain that Eyre, who sat as judge, was as eager to convict him, and as willing to abuse his office for that end, as Jeffreys or Scroggs were in their day. Those who differed widely enough from the prisoner, commented in plain terms on Eyre's charge and summing up.

The grand jury found a true bill against twelve members of the Corresponding Society. Hardy and Tooke were tried. The former was declared not guilty after an eight days', the latter after a six days' trial. The note from Joyce was proved to refer to a promise of selecting from the Court Calendar all the places held by the Grenvilles, the family now known more familiarly by the title of 'Buckingham.' Tooke was acquitted by the jury after a discussion of one minute, and was discharged amidst the cheers of an immense multitude. But he was gay and lively throughout his trial. On one of the days, as he was leaving the court, a lady admirer put a silk handkerchief round his neck to prevent his catching cold. 'Pray be careful, madam,' said he, ' I am rather ticklish, at present, about that particular place.'

Had Pitt succeeded in convicting Hardy and Tooke, he would have striven to extirpate all his opponents in the same way. This purpose was so well known at the time, that many fled from the risk to the United States. The acquittal of Tooke saved England from a reign of terror, and robbed informers and spies of half their perquisites. The reign of terror, however, was inaugurated in Ireland, where Protestant and Catholic rose against the detestable Government of the day, and Scotland suffered in the person of the martyrs to whom she had given the posthumous honour of a national memorial. Tooke might have used his victory against Pitt, but he forbore. He might perhaps have succeeded in making the heaven-born minister more unpopular; but if Pitt had quitted office, another of his school, or perhaps Fox, for whom Tooke had no respect whatever, would have succeeded. So when Pitt did resign, a far meaner and baser man followed in the person of Addington, for Addington never fell from generous purposes.

The imposition of the income-tax, then as now the most oppressive, dishonest, and immoral of all taxes, disclosed the poverty of Tooke's circumstances. He returned himself as worth only £60 a year. The clerk expressed his doubts as to the accuracy of the statement, and Tooke replied that 'the Act of Parliament has removed all the decencies which prevail among gentlemen, as it has given the commissioners, shrouded under the signature of their clerk, a right by law to tell me, that they have reason to believe that I am a liar.' So a subscription was entered into on his behalf, to which one person gave £1500. The county of Cornwall subscribed £2000. With the proceeds, an annuity of £600 was bought. Tooke had, besides, his house and grounds at Wimbledon, and a small estate at Brentford. Subsequently several considerable legacies were bequeathed to him, he became comparatively opulent, and was able to indulge his tastes in horticulture.

In 1797, he was again a candidate for Westminster. He had made up his differences with Fox, or at least did not oppose him. His rival was Sir Alan

Gardner, who stood in the Pitt interest. As was the custom of the time, the poll was continued from day to day, and the candidates addressed the electors as long as the contest was continued. On the second day, Tooke defined the policy of the Government with remarkable truth and pungency. 'Many have received a riband,' he said, 'from Pitt, for services which deserved a halter.' In answer to Gardner's protestations of loyalty, he said 'that his rival had two loves, the King and the Admiralty.' And when Gardner assured the crowd that he had left the Board, Tooke retorted that 'he is not the first admiral who after he has been divorced has married his lady again.' The Government made every effort and spared no cost to return Gardner. Fox was safe. But Tooke polled 2819 votes during the fifteen days' poll, his rival winning by 2005. It is something to say for Wilkes, that on the first day he gave Tooke his sole vote.

As before, no objection was taken by the candidates at Tooke's clerical antecedents. Had he been returned for Westminster, no notice would have been taken, and his seat, I am persuaded, would have been undisturbed. In February, 1801, Sir George Yonge vacated his seat at Old Sarum, by accepting the Chiltern Hundreds on his appointment as Governor of the Cape of Good Hope, and Tooke was returned in his place, on the nomination of Lord Camelford.

It is generally supposed that Old Sarum was a mere nomination borough. This is not quite correct.

At that time, it had an electoral roll of six. That Lord Camelford influenced this borough is unquestionable, though there is no reason to believe that his influence was much more absolute than local authority now is in such boroughs as Woodstock, Stamford, Enniskillen, and Bandon. But Tooke had all his life declaimed against the existence of these representative shams. The cardinal clause in his political creed was that taxation and representation should go together,—a position which, when pressed to its logical conclusion, would constrain the adoption of electoral districts, if it did not give a colour to the argument that the franchise should be multiplied in the case of those who pay most taxes. It appears, however, in justification of Tooke, that he accepted the seat at the strong solicitation of Lord Camelford, who did not persuade him till he had argued with him for three days and no small part of three nights.

He was introduced to the House, and shook hands with the Speaker, Mitford, afterwards Lord Redesdale. But Earl Temple, son of the Marquis of Buckingham, gave notice that he should, if no petition against the return was presented within a fortnight, inquire into the question of his eligibility. Meanwhile the member for Old Sarum took part in the business of the House; supported Mr. Sturt's abortive motion for an inquiry into the conduct of the Ferrol expedition; was astonished that ministers should resist an investigation into so gross a failure, and yet find time to sit in judgment on Old Sarum and the representative eligibility of an old priest; asked what kind of contagious malady was likely to affect them by his presence; and argued that a guarantee of thirty years must have been sufficient to guard against the infection of his original character.

Temple would not use his admissions, but proceeded to prove Tooke's ordination and his institution to the chapelry of New Brentford. The Sarum register was produced, and Wilson, the clerk of New Brentford, was summoned to prove that Tooke had officiated at this church. The latter motion was resisted, but was carried by 150 votes to 66, Erskine having been one of the tellers for the minority.

A select committee was now appointed to search for precedents as to the eligibility of clergymen to sit in the House of Commons. It was notorious that many had sat, that others besides Tooke were sitting in the House at the time during which Tooke was a member. The committee, however, made a report, which, though stupid and blundering, was honest. The strongest case against the right was that of a Dr. Craddock, who was rejected as ineligible in the first Parliament after the Restoration. The strongest case for the right was that of Mr. Rushworth, member for Yarmouth, Isle of Wight, who had sat in the Parliaments of 1780 and 1782; and, having been petitioned against in the last-named election as ineligible, had been seated by a committee. This case had the force of a precedent, and had undoubtedly been considered to settle the question.

Temple had sufficient reasons for disliking Tooke. His family had grown rich upon public money, as other families of nobility and influence have before and since. It had been proved on the trial of Tooke that Joyce's mysterious note had reference to the prodigal grants which had been heaped on the Grenvilles, and to Tooke's determination to collect and expose them. And thus, when Temple avowed among his motives for prosecuting the inquiry that he had a stake in the country, Tooke was able to answer very significantly, 'Why, so have I; but it is not stolen from the public hedge.'

The solitary argument on which the opponents of Tooke's seat could rely, was the fact that at certain periods certain clergymen had been declared incapable of sitting in the House of Commons 'because they had a voice in Convocation.' The meaning of this objection is as follows. The House of Commons and the House of Convocation were both summoned in order to assess themselves to grants of money for the king's use. Neither assembly had originally any legislative powers. But the House of Commons gradually, through petitions which asked the king's assent to such reforms in the law as seemed desirable, coupled their grants with the rectification of abuses, and ultimately asserted their right to an initiative in legislation. Still the primary business of both Houses was the grant of money. The House of Convocation rarely got beyond this position, except in times when the Tudor kings found it convenient to employ the clerical House for the purpose of enacting ecclesiastical laws, a proceeding which the Convocation of George the First's reign strove to develope into the right of passing judicial sentence on a bishop, the celebrated Hoadley. As a consequence of this innovation, Convocation was suppressed, and never met, except formally, for near a century and a half.

A beneficed clergyman, in right of his benefice, voted for a member of Convocation, and could himself sit; but he could not in this right vote for a member of the House of Commons and sit in the House of Commons himself. But a clergyman, beneficed or not, who possessed other such taxable property as gave him the franchise, could vote for a member of the House of Commons, and could sit there, if elected and properly qualified. That he did so sit is notorious, and, were the means of identifying such persons forthcoming, there cannot be a doubt that many would be discoverable. As it is, we know by accident that in early times such a person as Haxey was a clergyman, and did sit. An ecclesiastical estate could be taxed by Convocation only, a lay estate by the House of Commons only. It is true that the House of Commons sometimes taxed clerical fees, as in the notable example of assessments to the poor-rate; but subsidies to the monarch were invariably granted by each estate separately, the House of Commons confirming or annulling clerical grants. The motive of this control is manifest. It was to prevent the clergy from aiding the king against what the Commons might conceive to be the public good.

Soon after the Restoration, Archbishop Sheldon entered into an arrangement by which the ancient form of granting money was abandoned. Ever since that time the beneficed clergy vote, in virtue of their benefices, for members of the House of Commons, at first tacitly, though in later times the right has been formally recognised. As a consequence, they became capable of sitting as well as voting. No example, to be sure, is known of any beneficed clergyman sitting, but it was notorious that unbeneficed clergymen did. 'Several such persons,' says Hatsell, 'did sit; among others, I very well remember Mr. Gordon of Rochester, and several besides.' Hence, when Rushworth's case came on, the committee of the House of Commons took no notice of his opponents' objection, but declared him duly elected. These arguments, and such as these, must have been present to Tooke's mind, when he said that the lawyers were not agreed as to the meaning of the precedent.

Tooke, however, dwelt upon other objections to Temple's proceeding which were equally constitutional with that which I have alleged. 'Is,' he asked, 'the Canon law binding on the House of Commons?' He well knew that the House had solemnly affirmed that it was not binding on the laity. 'Is it binding on a clergyman when in and out of his profession, or does not the very act of declining to follow that calling exempt him from its authority? Is it possible for one

who has taken orders again to become one of the laity? And, lastly, if a clergyman does sit in the House of Commons, does he "use himself as a layman?"'
'For,' said Tooke, 'the Canon law says, "A clergyman shall not bear arms, shall not undertake a civil magistracy, and shall not use himself as a layman." Now,' he continued, 'you have many clergymen in the volunteers, many in the commission of the peace. You do not, therefore, think that these canons are binding on the clergy. Besides, the canons themselves treat of the deposition of priests. Now, what is a deposed priest? If the sentence makes him cease to be a clergyman, which must be conceded, does he not necessarily become a layman? If,' he concluded, 'I had committed such offences as would have degraded me from my order, I should be here unchallenged. My crime is my innocence; my only guilt is that of not having scandalized the order I once belonged to. I am in the situation of the young woman who asked for admission into the Magdalen. When questioned as to her previous history, it appeared that her life had been irreproachable. "Go about your business," said the authorities; "you must qualify before you come here."'

It would have been impossible for the House of Commons to have come, corrupt and vindictive as it was, to a decision adverse to Tooke's seat, on the intrinsic merits of the case, and defended as it was by every Whig of eminence in the House. But there was another means of settling the business. So Addington, to the surprise of all, moved the previous question, promising to remedy the abuse by a general measure. He was as good as his word. In a few days he brought in a Bill, which recited that doubts had arisen as to the eligibility of persons in holy orders to a seat in the House of Commons; and to remove them, enacted that no such person should hereafter sit, under the usual penalties. Tooke's seat was, however, preserved during the existing Parliament. The Bill was opposed at every stage in the Lower House by Fox and the Whigs. Rushworth petitioned against it. In committee words were added, extending its operation to ministers of the Church of Scotland. It passed the Lords without a division and without difficulty, on the plea that the Lords had nothing to do with the eligibility of the members of the Lower House, though not without a protest from Thurlow, who spoke of the ministry being affected by personal antipathies, and legislating against an individual. After the Bill became law, Tooke did not appear again in the House. He addressed, however, the electors of Westminster, and said, 'that something mysterious, miraculous, and supernatural had deprived him at the close of his life of the common rights of a man and a citizen; that he considered it a great compliment to him to be specially excluded from that Parliament in which Mr. Christopher Atkinson was an undisputed and welcome member; and presented his ironical thanks to Addington; for,' he concluded, 'had he proposed to hang me in the lobby, the same majority would have followed him.'

The contrast between his own case and that of Mr. Christopher Atkinson was natural and instructive. This fellow was a corn-factor, and was returned in 1780 as Member of Parliament for Hedon in Yorkshire, one of those rotten boroughs which were extinguished by the first Reform Act. He had entered into an arrangement to supply the victualling department of the navy with wheat, malt, and peas, on a commission of 6*d.* a quarter over the market price. He charged the public at the rate of seven or eight shillings for his services, probably by one of those collusions with the officials of the Admiralty, which have apparently been traditions of that office up to very recent times. He was unearthed and exposed by a Mr. William Bennett, a corn-dealer at Battersea, who dared him to prosecute. Atkinson filed certain affidavits, asserting his integrity. On this, Bennett prosecuted him for perjury, and obtained a conviction in November 1783. The culprit immediately absconded, and was, after a faint opposition on the part of Wilkes, Gascoigne, and Bramber, expelled the House, on December 4 of the same year. But in 1796, he was returned for Hedon again, and sat through this Parliament and that of 1802, when, under the name of Savile, he gave most discreditable evidence in an action for bribery brought against one Mestaer, with whom he had united in contesting Hedon. In all probability, there was no greater rascal in the House of Commons than this fellow; none whose presence was more disgraceful to the House; no man certainly whose character was in stronger contrast to that of Tooke.

Thenceforward he took no part in public business. He always welcomed his old political friends, and, in particular, his principal Westminster supporters. He died on March 18, 1812, having nearly completed his 77th year. In the last year or two of his life, he prepared his coffin and his grave. The former was made of marble, and had been presented to him by Chantrey, who highly valued his friendship, and owed his first success as a sculptor to the admirable bust he had made of Tooke, and to the discrimination of Nollekens. For his monument, which he intended should be in his garden, he had prepared a short inscription,—'John Horne Tooke, late proprietor, and now occupier of this spot. Content and grateful.'

I have narrated the principal facts of Tooke's life in such detail, that little more need be said. But it will not, I think, be out of place to say a few words more on the legislation which silenced him, and on the part which he played in English history during his singularly active political career, a career which extended over forty years.

It has been said that the House of Commons can do anything except reverse a law of nature. It may be said, with equal truth, that no legislative body has ever before inflicted a disability on a whole profession, because it wished to avenge itself on one man; that none has ever ventured on asserting, that because a person has entered on a profession, he shall not only while he follows it, but when he abandons it, be liable to a perpetual civil disability; that no other representative body has written over the entrance to that occupation the stern warning of Dante's Inferno—

'Abandon hope, all ye who enter here.'

I am not, it will be observed, referring to the obligations into which a man enters with his conscience, or with the religion to which he belongs, for no power on earth can perpetuate these obligations, or even extend them beyond a voluntary acquiescence in their force. But I refer to the fact, that the State in this country has carried far beyond any assumption which the most despotic arrogance has ventured on, the annexation of an inalienable status to the members of a particular profession. It has affirmed, by this remarkable law, more than any pope has ever asserted—the perpetual alienation of a civil right from a whole social order. The English law has deprived monastic vows of all validity, and yet it makes an act of religion more stringent and more absolute in its effects on the civil status of a man, than any monastic obligation of the severest Roman rule.

To this it may be objected, that the disability of Horne Tooke's Act, perpetually excluding all clergymen of the English and Scotch Establishments from a seat in the House of Commons, is a trifling matter, a grievance which is rarely felt, a mere sentiment. All this may be true. Bt it is a gross error in political science to imagine that the effects of affirming a great constitutional principle, by the highest constitutional authority, is to be estimated by its immediate incidence. Probably, not one clergyman in ten thousand cares a jot for Horne Tooke's Act; probably not one in a thousand knows of its existence.

But he knows, with greater or less distinctness, that the statute law of the land has made him a separate civil order, a particular caste. Now he must be so, while he exercises his functions for the Church in which he is enrolled—for this is a matter of social decency, just as every profession has its private code of conduct and honour. Beyond this, a Church cannot retain him; nor, if he declines to entertain the tenets, or carry on the ministry of that Church, will the Church care to retain him. But if the State does so, he inevitably sets up a claim to something more than he could otherwise achieve. For, I repeat, in every country whenever a disability is laid on any class of persons, it is invariably compensated, either directly or indirectly, by some privilege.

The Roman Church, it is true, conceived that a supernatural element was induced on ministers of religion at their ordination. She exalted the ceremony into a sacrament, and imposed various obligations on those who had received it. But, however rigid have been the rules with which Rome has surrounded her servants or subjects, she has always provided an escape from their incidence on individuals by the easy process of papal dispensation. That the Anglican Church at the Reformation did not assign any such virtue to ordination—did not pretend that it was indelible, is manifest from the fact that she repudiated the sacramental character of the office. It is equally notorious, too, that persons who had not received episcopal ordination were permitted to officiate in English churches for some time after the Reformation. It is in the Laudian epoch that the doctrine of sacerdotalism is particularly insisted on. The Church of the Reformation was rather disposed to adopt the adage of the enthusiastic Tertullian, 'Are not the laity also priests? So much so, that when no ecclesiastical officer is present, thou offerest the Eucharist and baptizest, and art by thyself a priest to thyself?' The grace of Church membership was conceived to be so great, that the difference between the minister of the Gospel and the disciple was dwarfed into nothingness.

I have little, indeed, no doubt, that the passing of Horne Tooke's Act has given an enormous impulse to official sacerdotalism. I am not referring to any authority freely given to those who can claim influence over their fellow-men, an influence which must be wisely employed by those who have won such influence. The hope of civilisation, the progress and perpetuation of religion, are equally effected by the power which wise and holy minds exercise over those other minds with which they are brought in contact. But I am referring to the power which is wielded by the function and not by the man, by the office and not by the character. The extension of this kind of lower influence might naturally be expected from a legal status such as that which I have referred to, and I can confidently appeal to the present claims of nearly every order of ministers in every Church, in support of the view which I entertain. When a great nation like our own has accepted so pronounced a principle, that a particular profession is incradicable and indelible, the example is infectious, the effect on the minds of those who can adopt the principle for sinister purposes is intelligible, and the most violent contest between the liberty of free thought and the claims of sacerdotalism may be anticipated. On the issues of such a contest, I have no wish to dilate. *Videte; judicate.* This, at least, is certain, that the struggle has commenced, and that the very fact of the struggle is disastrous.

There is not a public man in the eighteenth century who stands higher as an example of political morality than Tooke does. Disentangle him from his original profession, imagine him, as he always imagined himself, a layman in all civil matters, a citizen in public life, though to a small number of people a parish clergyman; and I dare venture on asserting, that the latter half of the eighteenth century shows no brighter public character. His estimate of characters and facts was equally just. His two famous quarrels were with men who had been allied to him, but from whom he broke away, because he held strongly to the rule, that the promotion of the public good cannot be expected from profligates and gamblers; that a man who is enslaved to low vices can never aid public morality. That he had a standing quarrel with the corruption and venality of the time, and with the parties who profited by it, was to be expected. It was to his honour that this quarrel was perpetual, and that he suffered nearly thirty years of political persecution because he confronted wholesale political dishonesty. It is possible that the treatment which he received from his generation made him bitter, defiant, and contemptuous; but very few men are able to preserve absolute serenity in the midst of a mob of rapacious knaves.

His action on public questions was almost invariably just and public-spirited. After the fever fit of admiration for the worthless idol of his youth, when he wrote and said things which were discreditable and foolish, he was as intelligent as he was firm. His conduct in the affair of the brothers Kennedy, of Doyle and Valline, his assistance to the Corporation of London in their memorable interview with the King, the aid he obtained for Bingley the printer, his controversy with Junius, his criticism on the American war, his attitude towards the revolutionary party in England, and his persistent maintenance of constitutional principles, were in the highest sense praiseworthy. His abilities, too, were as conspicuous as his public character. Had he gained his call to the bar, he would, beyond doubt, have speedily been reckoned one of the highest legal authorities, as he certainly was in his own trials one of the most powerful advocates. His acute discrimination was illustrated by the ingenuity of his philological theories, in days when philology was in its infancy.

His sense of personal honour was as high as his public character. He never betrayed the poverty which persecution reduced him to, though he received the assistance of his friends with dignity. Calumny made something of his relations with William Tooke; but this man publicly declared that he had made him his heir, and was perpetually leading him, not at Tooke's solicitation, to incur expenses, which he declared he would reimburse—promises which, from very avarice, he failed to fulfil. And once, when in a fit of senile pettishness, the old man said he would send for his nephew, Mr. Harwood, to succeed him, Horne Tooke told him that he could never meet him again, if he did not bring that gentleman, of whom he had now heard for the first time. Mr. Harwood came, and eventually succeeded to William Tooke's estate. John Tooke was no legacy hunter.

The history of the eighteenth century has been treated too much as though it were a gallery of family portraits, to which events are the mere frames. Public life, to be sure, was at that time a Homeric battle, in which a few prominent figures occupied the scene, and, I must add, divided the spoils. Among them there was one man who got no spoils, was always in earnest, always serious. 'The Parson,' said Wilkes, 'never laughs.' He was also patriotic and wise. He swam against the current which he could not stem. It is, perhaps, still impossible to forget him as the Vicar of New Brentford; but though his enemies called him a hoary traitor, and even his friends thought it necessary to apologise for him, as a retired clergyman, they who are willing to be just to one of the foremost men of his age, will find much that is wholesome in the career of the politician and philosopher of Wimbledon.

www.ingramcontent.com/pod-product-compliance
Lightning Source LLC
Chambersburg PA
CBHW032227230426
43666CB00033B/1625